WITHDRAWN
Congressional
Campaign Finances

Congressional Campaign Finances

History, Facts, and Controversy

I.C.C. LIBRARY

CONGRESSIONAL QUARTERLY, INC.
WASHINGTON, D.C.

Photos: R. Michael Jenkins

Copyright © 1992
Congressional Quarterly
1414 22nd Street, N.W.
Washington, D.C. 20037

Printed in the United States of America

Library of Congress Cataloging-in-Publication Data

Congressional campaign finances : history, facts, and controversy.
    p. cm.
    Includes bibliographical references and index.
    ISBN 0-87187-626-4
    1. Campaign funds--United States. 2. Campaign funds--United States--History. I. Congressional Quarterly Inc.
    JK1991.C658 1992
    324.7'8'0973--dc20   92-2748
                                CIP

Editor: Mary W. Cohn
Contributors: Kerry Kern, Nancy Kervin, John L. Moore, Patricia Ann O'Connor, Jenny K. Philipson
Book Design: Kaelin Chappell

CONTENTS

Preface

In 1991 the House and the Senate each passed campaign finance reform bills. If the chambers can settle the differences between the two measures in 1992, they will send to the president the first major overhaul of congressional campaign finance since the 1974 post-Watergate reforms.

The battle to regulate and reform the way elections are financed has been ongoing since the early part of this century. Various measures have been passed over the years: the 1907 Tillman Act, the Federal Corrupt Practices acts of 1910 and 1925, and the Federal Election Campaign Act (FECA) of 1971. Perhaps the most significant reform measure was the FECA Amendments of 1974. This law was a reaction to the campaign abuses brought to light by the Watergate scandal.

Although the 1974 act and the subsequent 1976 and 1979 FECA amendments tightened up campaign finance law, problems still remained. Congress considered various proposals throughout the 1980s, but it was not until the latter part of that decade that Congress got down to business. The reason? Image problems that were creating a wave of resentment against and frustration with Congress.

The Keating Five scandal exposed how campaign contributions can govern behavior in Congress. Polls showed that most Americans believe members of Congress are more interested in serving special interests than constituents. Voters, seemingly incapable of turning out incumbents at the polls, began toying with term limits. President George Bush in his 1991 State of the Union address asked Congress to ban political action committees. New pressure groups joined a grassroots battle to force action. Even on Capitol Hill, a rising chorus has decried the very financial system that most members wear like a comfortable old shoe.

Given these signs, it was no surprise that leaders of both parties hoisted campaign finance legislation to the top of their agendas in Congress.

How This Book Is Organized

Congressional Campaign Finances covers all aspects of campaign finance, from efforts to reform the system to the amounts of contributions allowed by law.

Chapter 1 provides an overview of the campaign financing system and explains why campaign finance reform has been such a heated and divisive issue.

Campaign contributions and expenditures are discussed in Chapter 2. This chapter explains the sources of contributions, including individuals, candidates themselves, political action committees, party committees, and independent organizations, and how much each may contribute. Also covered is how much candidates spend on an election and where the money goes.

Chapter 3 describes the problems in the campaign financing system, such as the high cost of campaigns and the advantages of incumbency. Also covered are the various proposals for changing the system and why Democrats and Republicans have such a different approach to the problem.

The historical development of curbing the abuses associated with financing campaigns is covered in Chapter 4. Chapter 5 covers campaign finance reforms enacted in the 1970s, and the final chapter deals with reform proposals in the 1980s and 1990s.

An appendix includes the texts of several major campaign finance laws and the historic *Buckley v. Valeo* Supreme Court decision, which upheld limits on campaign contributions set by the 1974 Federal Election Campaign Act Amendments, but struck down the law's limits on campaign spending as a violation of First Amendment rights.

The material in *Congressional Campaign Finances* first appeared in *Guide to Congress,* 4th ed. Information on the campaign finance bills passed in the 102nd Congress was updated for this volume.

CHAPTER 1

The Campaign Financing System:

Widespread Dissatisfaction

In the early years of the twentieth century Congress attempted to devise a system to limit the influence of money in politics. In the closing decade of the century Congress was still at it.

Although campaign finance had changed dramatically over the century—from its early freewheeling days to a heavily regulated system—the public demands for reform in the early 1900s and in the early 1990s were much the same: to curb the ability of interest groups and wealthy individuals to dominate the flow of campaign money and to try to establish level playing fields for challengers as well as incumbents, for politicians of modest means as well as wealthier campaigners.

The costs of elections had spiraled upward in modern times. The price tag for the 1990 congressional elections was $445 million.[1] Members of Congress were finding themselves under relentless pressure to raise funds for their campaigns—a time-consuming task that critics said was taking its toll not only on the members personally but on Congress as an institution.

But, judging from the electoral success of congressional incumbents, the campaign financing system was paying off for members. The reelection rate in 1990 for members of the Senate was 96.9 percent and 96 percent for House members. Some reformers decried the system for producing what they saw as a "permanent Congress" and pointed a finger at interest groups' political action committees (PACs) and their overwhelming support for incumbents. Others dismissed such claims.

Consensus Elusive

Wide dissatisfaction with the system became increasingly obvious in the 1980s. But there was no consensus in Congress on what was wrong with the system, let alone what would make it right.

For every person who expressed dismay at the skyrocketing campaign costs, there was someone who said the costs were small when compared with a major corporation's advertising budget or the price tag of a nuclear submarine. For everyone who called for limits on campaign spending, there was someone who charged that limits would only further entrench incumbents and disadvantage challengers. For everyone who deplored the role of special interest money and PACs in American politics, there was someone who defended them as a manifestation of democracy's pluralism. For everyone who saw public money as the way to eliminate outside influences in politics, there was someone who scoffed at its use in times of $300 billion deficits.

Beyond specific policy disagreements was the less tangible love-hate relationship legislators had with the system. Members were faced with the dilemma of having to change a system that returned the vast majority of them to the halls of Congress election after election. As reform advocate Sen. Robert C. Byrd, D-W.Va., put it in 1991: "We are afraid to let go of the slick ads and the high-priced consultants, afraid to let go of the PAC money and the polls, unsure that we want to change the rules of the game that we all understand and know so well." [2]

Reformers faced the enormous task of proposing legislation that would bridge the differences between Democrat and Republican, representative and senator, incumbent and challenger. Members were afraid of the unknowns that surrounded change—how each party would adapt to it and whether it might give the opposing party an advantage. Democrats feared Republican proposals to enhance the financial role of political parties, a GOP strength, and to curb PACs and regulate political activity by labor unions, two sources of Democratic strength. Republicans feared that Democratic proposals for spending caps could make it harder for the GOP to retake control of Congress. And opinion split in all directions on using tax dollars to finance congressional campaigns. Further complicating matters were the differing needs of the two chambers. Individual contributions were of much greater importance to senators than to representatives, while PAC dollars made a difference in House races but not as much in Senate campaigns.

Assuming a bill could be moved through Congress, it would then face the hurdle of White House approval. In the early 1990s various proposals of the Democratic Congress routinely invited veto threats from the Republican president. And

---

Party Views of Campaign Spending Limits

"One thing is clear: The only meaningful way to reform Senate elections is to have limits on campaign spending."

—Senate Democratic leader
George J. Mitchell, Maine

"For the last three years, Democrats have been trying to sell the concept of spending limits as the only way to reform the campaign finance laws. Let me tell senators why they are doing this—because it serves the partisan interests of the Democratic party."

—Sen. Mitch McConnell, R-Ky.

"We provide for real reform by providing for a limit on overall spending."

—Sen. David L. Boren, D-Okla.

"An absolute, fixed cap on campaign spending is nothing more than a prescription for incumbency protection."

—Senate Republican leader
Bob Dole, Kansas

Source: Congressional Quarterly Weekly Report, May 26, 1990, 1622.

---

even if the two branches could find common ground for legislative agreement, there was still the third branch to contend with. The memory of the Supreme Court knocking out key portions of a major campaign finance measure in the 1970s was still fresh.

Pressure for Reform

Public attention was riveted on the flaws of the campaign finance system in 1990 by the investigation into the so-called Keating Five—five senators suspected of doing favors for a wealthy campaign contributor, Charles H. Keating, Jr. The controversy, an offshoot of the savings and loan scandal, added fuel to a fire that Common Cause, a public interest lobby, had lit under Congress to revise the way members financed their campaigns.

At the heart of the Keating Five scandal was $1.5 million in contributions made or solicited by Keating, the powerful owner of a thrift and real estate empire, for the campaigns or other political causes of the five senators. More than half of the money—$850,000—was paid out of corporate funds to nonprofit voter registration organizations with which one of the senators, Alan Cranston, D-Calif., was affiliated. Keating also employed a technique called "bundling," through which he raised many individual contributions from family members, associates, and employees of his companies and handed the contributions over in a lump sum designed to impress the recipient politicians. Televised hearings and news stories revealing Keating's use of his fund-raising skills to assemble clout in Washington proved far more effective at raising questions about the relationship between elected officials and major contributors than the flood of statistics about PACs that were issued by good-government groups.

Further pressure was placed on Congress by public opinion polls such as a CBS News/New York Times poll conducted a month before the November 1990 elections that found 71 percent of those surveyed agreeing that "most members of Congress are more interested in serving special interest groups than the people they represent."

Both chambers passed bills in 1990, over GOP objections, but action came late in the session and the bills died when Congress adjourned and went home for the elections.

The pressure was on again in 1991. As the 102nd Congress began, the Senate Ethics Committee was still considering the Keating case. Many House incumbents had seen their winning vote margins narrowed in the November election. President George Bush in his State of the Union address asked Congress to ban political action committees. New pressure groups were joining a grass-roots battle to force action. By the end of 1991, both the Senate and the House had passed reform bills, with a conference scheduled for 1992. Because the bills differed greatly on critical issues, how the House and Senate would resolve the differences was anyone's guess. The only certainty was that anything approaching comprehensive legislation would provoke a bruising battle both in and between the two chambers, and possibly between Capitol Hill and the White House, if it got that far.

The battle would be a familiar one. As Common Cause president Fred Wertheimer once put it: "There are no fights like campaign finance fights because they are battles about the essence of politics and power." [3]

Ongoing Search for Solutions

Attempts to reform the campaign finance system were nothing new.

Campaign finance reformers over the years have sought to curb campaign spending by limiting and regulating campaign expenditures and donations made to candidates as well as by informing voters of the amounts and sources of the donations, and the amounts, purposes, and recipients of the expenditures. Disclosure was intended to reveal which candidates, if any, were unduly indebted to interest groups, in time to forewarn the voters.

Congress had argued the issues of campaign finance since the first law regulating campaigns was enacted during the administration of Theodore Roosevelt. Major new laws, however, came only after scandals: Teapot Dome in the 1920s, Watergate in the 1970s.

In 1925 the Teapot Dome scandal yielded the Federal Corrupt Practices Act, an extensive statute governing the conduct of federal campaigns. That act codified earlier laws limiting campaign expenditures, but the limits were so unrealistically low and the law so riddled with loopholes that it was ineffectual.

Watergate, though, changed all that. The June 1972 break-in at Democratic national headquarters in Washington's Watergate office building touched off a scandal that became the 1970s' code word for governmental corruption. Although the scandal had many aspects, money in politics was at its roots. Included in Watergate's catalog of misdeeds were specific violations of campaign spending laws, violations of other criminal laws facilitated by the availability of virtually unlimited campaign contributions, and still other instances where campaign funds were used in a manner that strongly suggested influence peddling.

Congress had begun to move on campaign finance even before Watergate. Less than six months before the break-in, Congress had adopted two pieces of legislation containing some of the ground rules under which elections were conducted into the 1990s. First, Congress approved legislation allowing a $1 tax checkoff to finance presidential campaigns. Congress also passed the Federal Election Campaign Act (FECA), requiring comprehensive disclosure of campaign contributions and expenditures by candidates for federal office and placing a limit on the amount of money candidates could spend on media advertising. (The media spending limits were repealed in 1974.) The 1971 FECA ultimately had a limited impact on controlling campaign spending.

But Watergate focused public attention on campaign spending at all levels of government and produced a mood in Congress that even the most reluctant legislators found difficult to resist. In the aftermath came the most significant overhaul in campaign finance legislation in the nation's history. Major legislation passed in 1974 (the House had passed its version on the day Richard Nixon had announced he would resign the presidency) and 1976, coming on the heels of the 1971 legislation,

radically altered the system of financing federal elections.

The FECA Amendments of 1974 set limits on contributions and expenditures for congressional and presidential elections, established an independent Federal Election Commission (FEC) to oversee federal elections laws, and created the framework for providing presidential candidates with public financing. The two years of debate that preceded passage of this law was, until 1990, the closest Congress had ever come to enacting public financing of congressional campaigns.

Before the sweeping 1974 act received its first real test, it was extensively pruned by the Supreme Court. The Court in its 1976 decision in *Buckley v. Valeo* (424 U.S. 1) upheld the FECA's disclosure requirements, contribution limitations, and public financing of presidential elections. But it struck down spending limits for congressional and presidential races, including restraints on the use of a candidate's personal assets, except for presidential candidates who accepted public financing. It also struck down limits on independent expenditures, expenditures made in support of or opposition to a candidate but without the knowledge or cooperation of the candidate.

The justices weighed First Amendment rights against the 1974 act's underlying purpose: prevention of the abuses that surfaced during Watergate. In the case of contributions, the Court concluded that First Amendment considerations were outweighed because "the quantity of communication by the contributor does not increase perceptibly with the size of his contribution." But it found limiting expenditures to be a "substantial" restraint on free speech that could preclude "significant use of the most effective modes of communication."

Many subsequent congressional efforts to change the campaign finance system were driven by the desire to find a way to limit congressional campaign spending without violating the mandates of the Court decision. With the ceilings on expenditures removed, campaign costs grew apace and candidates became increasingly dependent on raising money in the easiest and most cost-effective way—from PACs.

In striking down restraints on independent expenditures, the Supreme Court opened the door for individuals and PACs to spend millions of dollars independently; such spenders were generally derided by candidates and party leaders as unwelcome "loose cannons" in the political process. The decision spurred the rise of independent expenditures by nonconnected, or ideological, PACs. Sharply negative ads often underwritten by such groups gained the enmity of both parties.

In 1979 Congress amended the FECA to encourage more grass-roots and political party activity in federal campaigns. Included in the package of amendments was a section allowing state and local parties to underwrite voter-registration and get-out-the-vote drives in behalf of presidential tickets without regard to financial limits. Because this money could come from funds normally prohibited under federal election law—excessively large individual contributions, as well as direct corporate and labor union treasury money—it was not "hard" to raise and, therefore, was labeled "soft" money. As the use of soft money increased, critics charged that while national parties nominally used soft money to bolster state parties, the money effectively went to aid federal candidates. Such funds played an important role in the 1988 elections, and they became significant targets of proposed legislation by both parties in 1990.

Throughout the late 1970s reformers sought to extend public financing to congressional races, but their efforts failed. The post-Watergate mood in Congress was less amenable to further major changes in campaign financing, at least for the time being.

Both parties during the Reagan era debated public financing for congressional campaigns, but no significant legislation was passed. In 1987, with Democrats back in control of the Senate, Majority Leader Byrd decided to make campaign financing a major issue, but a public financing bill fell victim to a Republican filibuster and was shelved early in 1988.

As the 101st Congress convened in January 1989, charges of ethical violations and questionable financial dealings involving Speaker Jim Wright, D-Texas, intensified pressures on House Democrats to act on campaign finance legislation. Wright, facing charges that would lead to his resignation from Congress, embraced campaign finance reform and created a bipartisan task force to develop a reform plan. Legislation was introduced in the Senate, and President Bush offered a package of proposals as well. Momentum continued to build throughout the year in both chambers, but no legislation was passed.

And so the efforts at campaign finance reform spilled over into the 1990s. *(Details, p. 52)*

NOTES

1. Unless otherwise noted, the figures in this chapter on campaign receipts and expenditures in the 1990 elections were from the Federal Election Commission and include money that moved during the 1989-90 election cycle in all races, including those of primary losers. The main source was "1990 Congressional Election Spending Drops to Low Point," a Federal Election Commission press release of February 22, 1991. Other FEC press releases used included "PAC Activity Falls in 1990 Elections," March 31, 1991; and "FEC Releases Summary of 1989-90 Political Party Finances," March 15, 1991.

2. Quoted in Chuck Alston, "Image Problems Propel Congress Back to Campaign Finance Bills," *Congressional Quarterly Weekly Report*, February 2, 1991, 281.

3. Quoted in Larry J. Sabato, *PAC Power: Inside the World of Political Action Committees* (New York: W. W. Norton, 1984), 171.

CHAPTER 2

Congressional Campaigns:

Contributions and Expenditures

The modern congressional election is a complex financial affair. Finance chairmen, fund raisers, accountants, and a variety of consultants play crucial roles in today's campaigns. Decisions on how to raise money and how to marshal a campaign's resources can be key to electoral success.

Money pours in from a vast array of sources—not all of them controlled by the candidate—including individuals, candidates themselves and their families, PACs, party committees, and independent organizations running their own campaigns to influence the outcome. Money flows out for rent, computers, salaries, polls, consulting fees, printing, postage, and radio, television, and newspaper advertising.

Much of the money that at one time moved in the shadows of campaigns is now a matter of public record, thanks to the stringent disclosure provisions of the FECA. All candidates for federal office, once they cross a certain threshold, periodically must submit to the FEC itemized accounts of contributions and expenditures in excess of $200 and debts and obligations owed to or by the candidate or committee. These reports, which are made public by the FEC, provide a window on the modern political campaign.

POLITICAL CONTRIBUTIONS

FEC figures indicated that congressional candidates raised a total of $471 million during the 1989-90 election cycle. House and Senate incumbents together raised $300 million; challengers raised $102 million. An additional $68.6 million was raised by candidates for open seats.

When broken down by chamber, the figures showed that Senate candidates raised a total of $186 million, with incumbents attracting nearly $119 million, challengers $55 million, and open-seat candidates almost $13 million.

House candidates took in a total of nearly $285 million. The incumbents' share was $181 million, while challengers raised about $47.5 million and open-seat candidates brought in $56 million.

The bulk of this money came from two principal sources: individual contributions and PACs. Lesser amounts came from the political parties and from the candidates themselves.

Individual Contributions

Political campaigns have traditionally been financed by the contributions of individual donors.

Contribution Limits

Recipients

Donors	Candidate committee	Local party committee[1]	State party committee[1]	National party committee[2]	PAC[3]	Special limits
Individual	$1,000 per election[4]	$5,000 per year combined limit		$20,000 per year	$5,000 per year	$25,000 per year overall limit[5]
Local party committee[1] State party committee[1] (multicandidate)[6]	$5,000 per election combined limit	unlimited transfers to other party committees unlimited transfers to other party committees			$5,000 per year combined limit	
National party committee[2] (multicandidate)[6]	$5,000 per election	unlimited transfers to other party committees			$5,000 per year	$17,500 to Senate candidate per campaign[7]
PAC[3] (multicandidate)[6]	$5,000 per election	$5,000 per year combined limit		$15,000 per year	$5,000 per year	
PAC[3] (not multicandidate)	$1,000 per election	$5,000 per year combined limit		$20,000 per year	$5,000 per year	

1. A state party committee shares its limits with local party committees in that state unless a local committee's independence can be demonstrated.
2. A party's national committee, Senate campaign committee, and House campaign committee each have separate limits except for contributions to Senate candidates. See Special Limits column.
3. Affiliated PACs share the same set of limits on contributions received and made.
4. Each of the following is considered a separate election with a separate limit: primary election, caucus or convention with authority to nominate, general election, and special election.
5. A contribution to a party committee or a PAC counts against the annual limit for the year in which the contribution is made. A contribution to a candidate counts against the limit for the year of the election for which the contribution is made.
6. A multicandidate committee is a political committee that has been registered for at least six months, has received contributions from more than fifty contributors and, with the exception of a state party committee, has made contributions to at least five federal candidates.
7. This limit is shared by the national committee and the Senate campaign committee.

Source: Federal Election Commission.

The biggest difference today is that the pre-Watergate contributor of unlimited amounts of money—the "fat cat"—has been largely replaced by the smaller donor, who may give directly to a candidate or contribute through a political party committee or PAC. Under the FECA, individuals are limited to $1,000 per candidate per election (a primary election and the general election are considered separate elections with separate limits), $20,000 a year to a national party committee, and $5,000 a year to a PAC, with an overall annual limit of $25,000. As a result of these limits, elections once financed by thousands of people are now funded by contributions from millions of people. *(Contribution limits, chart, p. 8)*

Nonetheless, some concern has been expressed about the decline during the 1980s of small direct contributions to candidates. A 1990 study by the House Democratic Study Group (DSG) found that contributions of less than $200 grew at a significantly slower pace than other sources of campaign revenue, while contributions between $200 and $500 grew rapidly, and contributions of more than $500 grew even more rapidly. The report speculated that small donors may not have been able to keep pace financially with soaring campaign costs or other sources of campaign funds, or that perhaps it was no longer economically feasible to solicit small contributors and, as a result, candidates had focused their time and resources on contributors who could write large checks. Another possibility, the DSG report said, was that a number of small contributors may have decided that their interests could be better promoted through contributions to PACs instead of direct contributions to candidates.[1]

Direct individual contributions to 1990 congressional candidates amounted to $249.5 million, or 53 percent of their total receipts. A breakdown by chambers highlighted a key difference between Senate and House fund raising: individual contributions accounted for 64 percent ($119.6 million) of Senate candidates' receipts but only 46 percent ($129.9 million) of House candidates'.

Although scarcely used by individuals in congressional elections, an "independent expenditure" is another avenue for affecting elections. This is an expenditure for communications advocating the election or defeat of a candidate that is made without the knowledge or cooperation of the candidate or the candidate's campaign organization. Congress had placed a limit on such expenditures in the 1974 FECA amendments but this, along with most other limits, was thrown out by the Supreme Court in 1976 as a violation of First Amendment rights. PACs have used independent expenditures on a far larger scale than individual donors have, but a $1.1 million expenditure in 1984 by businessman Michael Goland urging the defeat of Sen. Charles Percy, R-Ill., reportedly because of his Middle East stance, highlighted the potential of such spending when Percy lost. Independent expenditures must be reported to the FEC when they exceed $250 per year.

Political Action Committees

Labor unions, corporations, and incorporated trade and membership organizations are prohibited by law from using their general treasury funds to make contributions or expenditures in federal elections. They, therefore, participate indirectly in the electoral process through what are called "separate segregated funds." These funds, along with the political committees of other organizations (such as ideological and issue groups) that raise money for candidates, are known as political action committees. Most PACs are permitted to contribute $5,000 per candidate per election, with no overall limit. They also may give $15,000 per year to a national party committee.

Although PACs have been around for some time—the Congress of Industrial Organizations (CIO) founded the first modern PAC in 1943—their significance has increased dramatically since the 1970s. The number of PACs registered with the FEC rose from 608 at the end of 1974 to 4,172 at the end of 1990. Of those PACs registered, 3,044 actually made contributions in the 1989-90 election cycle.

But the more telling statistics on PAC growth are those on PAC giving. In the 1977-78 election cycle, PACs contributed $34 million to congressional candidates; in the 1989-90 election cycle, they reported contributions of about $150 million. The top fifty contributors to all congressional candidates during the 1989-90 election cycle (including senators not up for reelection in 1990) ranged from the Realtors Political Action Committee, which gave $3.1 million, to the Philip Morris Political Action Committee, which gave $573,410.[2] The contributions of these fifty amounted to about 35 percent of the total reported by PACs.

In the period from the 1978 election to the 1988 election, PAC money as a percentage of Senate candidates' receipts (amounts raised by candidates and party expenditures on behalf of candidates) went from 13 percent to 22 percent. And in House elections the percentage of receipts attributed to PAC money rose from 24 percent in 1978 to 40 percent in 1988.[3]

Why this explosive growth in PAC numbers and dollars? The answer can be found in the reform legislation of the 1970s. In 1971 Congress sanctioned the use of regular corporate and union funds to pay the overhead costs of PACs. Legislation in 1974 placed more stringent limits on individual contributions than on those of PACs. That same year Congress also lifted restrictions on the formation of PACs by government contractors. Whenever reform struck another target, PACs benefited, according to political scientist Frank J. Sorauf, who said it illustrated a fundamental law of the mechanics of campaign finance: "Available money seeks an outlet, and if some outlets are narrowed or closed off, money flows with increased pressure to the outlets still open. It is the law that

systems of campaign finance share with hydraulic systems." [4]

Further impetus for growth came in 1975 when the FEC ruled that the Sun Oil Co. could establish a PAC and solicit contributions to SunPAC from stockholders and employees; the ruling eliminated the last barrier that had prevented corporations from forming PACs. FEC figures show that the number of corporate PACs jumped from 139 at the time of the SunPAC ruling in November 1975 to 433 by the end of 1976. PACs also reaped benefits from the Supreme Court's 1976 decision striking down restrictions on independent spending. *(SunPAC case, p. 48)*

The rapid growth of PAC money and influence in the electoral process has generated much controversy. Defenders of PACs have insisted they are an outgrowth of a democratic society. "PACs are both natural and inevitable in a free, pluralist democracy," political scientist Larry J. Sabato wrote. "In fact, the vibrancy and health of a democracy depend in good part on the flourishing of interest groups and associations among its citizenry." [5]

But critics have branded PACs as a source of tainted money because their giving often has been tied to specific legislation or to a leadership position or to membership on a certain committee or to the mere fact of incumbency. Wertheimer of Common Cause told the Senate Rules Committee: "It is increasingly clear that PAC participation represents a threat to the public trust in the integrity of our electoral and congressional decision-making processes." [6]

Public opinion polls have indicated a distrust of PACs among voters. A 1991 study by the Library of Congress's Congressional Research Service (CRS) reported that various polls had found that between 57 and 81 percent of registered or likely voters had negative perceptions of PACs as a corrupting influence on Congress and that a majority supported the idea that candidates for high federal office should not be allowed to accept PAC funds.[7]

Who Paid the Bills of 1988 Winners

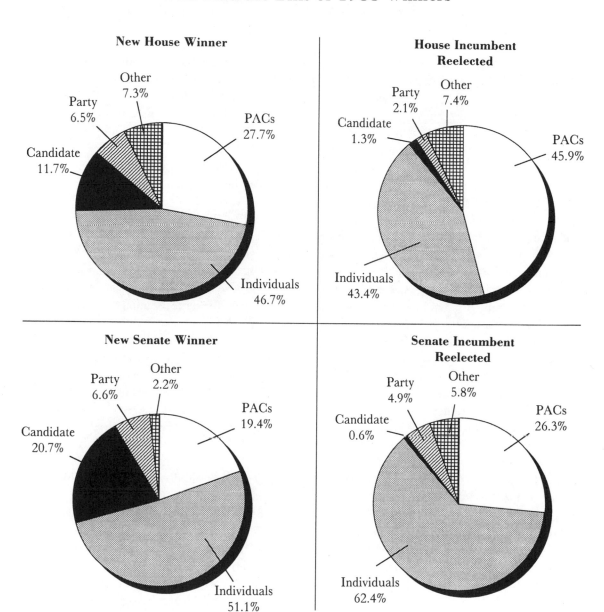

New House Winner

Other 7.3%
Party 6.5%
Candidate 11.7%
PACs 27.7%
Individuals 46.7%

House Incumbent Reelected

Party 2.1%
Other 7.4%
Candidate 1.3%
PACs 45.9%
Individuals 43.4%

New Senate Winner

Party 6.6%
Other 2.2%
Candidate 20.7%
PACs 19.4%
Individuals 51.1%

Senate Incumbent Reelected

Party 4.9%
Other 5.8%
Candidate 0.6%
PACs 26.3%
Individuals 62.4%

Source: Larry Makinson, *Open Secrets: The Dollar Power of PACs in Congress* (Washington, D.C.: Center for Responsive Politics/Congressional Quarterly, 1990), 3.

One member of Congress who renounced PAC contributions said he thought PACs symbolized why voters had become alienated from politics. "People feel like it's big money, big business, big labor, the lobbyists who are represented, that little by little the playing field has been tilted," Romano L. Mazzoli, D-Ky., stated in 1990.[8]

While views on PACs were enormously diverse, certain facts about them were beyond dispute. One was that PACs were overwhelmingly incumbent-oriented. FEC figures showed that of the more than $150 million that candidates reported receiving from PACs during the 1990 campaign, about $116.6 million went to incumbents, but only $16 million to challengers and $18 million to open-seat candidates. PAC contributions were far more significant in the House than in the Senate: nearly $110 million went to House candidates and $41 million to Senate candidates. And more money went to Democrats ($93.5 million) than to Republicans ($57 million).

Few have contended that PACs were out to buy votes with these contributions, but rather that their aim was to buy access to members in positions to help—or hinder—their cause. That philosophy or ideology was the overriding concern of PACs was illustrated by PAC giving to election winners after previously supporting the winner's opponent. A Congressional Quarterly study of postelection giving to the Senate class of 1986 found that 41 percent of the PAC money received came from groups who had previously contributed to the new senators' opponents and another 13 percent came from groups who had supported both sides in the election. "It's called 'correcting a mistake,'" explained Sabato, who said he heard the term from PAC managers while he was researching a book on PACs.[9]

Another example of PACs' incumbent preference was seen in the increasing contributions business PACs made to Democratic incumbents in the House during the 1980s. This increase was attrib-

uted to the persuasive powers of California Rep. Tony Coelho, chairman of the Democratic Congressional Campaign Committee in the early 1980s, who reportedly managed to convince traditionally conservative PACs of the logic of having access to a sitting member of the House instead of wasting money on a challenger who was likely to lose.[10] This trend led one group of observers to conclude: "Business groups have not changed their political stripes; they have all but dropped them." [11]

In addition to direct contributions to candidates, PACs also have made use of independent expenditures. PACs made independent expenditures of $3.5 million for congressional candidates in the 1990 races and some $600,000 against. The numbers were small compared to other facets of PAC spending but the potential for big expenditures did exist because there were no statutory limits on them. One often-cited example occurred in 1980 when the National Conservative Political Action Committee (NCPAC) spent more than $1 million against six liberal Senate incumbents, four of whom were defeated.

Although PACs are usually associated with interest groups outside Congress, a small but influential group of PACs called "leadership PACs" or "personal PACs" exists within Congress. These are separate PACs formed by members of Congress or other political leaders independent of their own campaign committees. They often are the PACs of presidential hopefuls, congressional leaders, or would-be leaders. "In almost all cases—and this is central to their role as brokers—sponsoring individuals are raising and giving money at least in part to support their own political careers, positions, or goals," Sorauf wrote.[12] These personal PACs often have rather nondescriptive names, so it is not easy to count them. Larry Makinson of the Center for Responsive Politics found that no fewer than fifty-five members of Congress—thirty Democrats and twenty-five Republicans—had formed or sponsored their own PACs during the 1987-88 election cycle. These PACs gave out more than $4.3 million of the total $4.9 million given by leadership PACs. (Much of the rest came from PACs run by George Bush and Ronald Reagan.) Leadership PAC giving declined sharply in 1990—as would be expected in a nonpresidential election year—when they gave less than $2.4 million, according to Makinson.[13]

Political Parties

Political parties provide direct assistance to candidates in two ways: through contributions and through payments to vendors in a candidate's behalf. Such payments, known as "coordinated expenditures," fund any number of campaign services such as polling, research, advertising, or buying TV time.

National committees, which include the party's national committee as well as House and Senate campaign committees, are each permitted to make contributions of $5,000 per candidate per election. That amounts to a total of $20,000 in party money for candidates' primary and general election races for the House, but for Senate candidates there is a $17,500 limit. State and local party committees may give a combined total of $5,000 per election.

Coordinated expenditures are made only in general elections, and the amount that can be spent is set by formula. For House candidates in states with more than one member, the limit is $10,000, adjusted for inflation, which translated into a $25,140 limit in 1990. For House candidates in states with only one member, the parties may spend up to the limit for Senate candidates in those states, which in 1990 was $50,280. For Senate candidates, the party committees could spend the greater of either $20,000, adjusted for inflation—$50,280 in 1990—or two cents for every person of voting age, again adjusted for inflation. According to this formula, possible coordinated expenditures

for Senate candidates in 1990 ranged from the base figure of $50,280 in the less populous states to nearly $1.1 million in California.

The Republican party has proven itself to be the more successful fund raiser of the two parties. In the 1989-90 election cycle, Republican party committees raised a total of $207.2 million and spent $214.2 million. Of this, they contributed $2.9 million to congressional candidates and made coordinated expenditures of $10.7 million. The bulk of the money the party raises goes for party-building, electoral, and fund-raising activities.

Democrats raised a total of $86.7 million and spent $92.1 million. They contributed $1.5 million to congressional candidates and spent $8.6 million in their behalf.

These contributions and expenditures constitute a comparatively small percentage of the overall receipts of candidates, but the parties also help candidates in other ways. Parties can raise unlimited amounts of so-called soft money—essentially unregulated money—from unions, corporations, trade associations, and individuals for state and local party activities. Although this money cannot

by law be used for federal candidates, when it is channeled into such grass-roots activities as voter registration, education, and turnout, party candidates at all levels benefit.

The largest amounts of soft money have been raised during presidential election cycles. The Citizens' Research Foundation estimated that $45 million in soft money was raised and spent during the 1988 elections.[14] But substantial amounts also have been raised during midterm elections. A study by the Center for Responsive Politics found that more than $25 million was collected in the 1989-90 election cycle—$18.5 million by the Republicans and $6.6 million by the Democrats. The study found forty contributions of $100,000 or more.[15]

Reports on soft money in the past have been based largely on voluntary disclosures; however, at the beginning of 1991, regulations went into effect requiring that the money be reported to the FEC and the reports made available to the public.

Political parties also like to act as conduits, passing contributions through their committees to candidates. Thanks to sophisticated computers and mass mailings, a party can target those who might be interested in a race and encourage them to contribute. Through a practice called "earmarking," a contributor can direct money to a candidate or committee through an intermediary, such as the party.

Computers and such techniques as electronic bank drafts have also facilitated the practice of "bundling," in which checks from a number of contributors are grouped together and presented as a package to a candidate. For bundling to be legal, however, the original donors must retain control over designation of the eventual recipient. A federal judge in 1991 ruled in a lawsuit brought by Common Cause that the National Republican Senatorial Committee (NRSC) broke federal election law with a 1986 fund-raising scheme that raised $2.3 million for twelve Republican Senate candidates. The judge ruled that the NRSC, rather than the donors, exercised control over who the recipients would be and therefore the $2.3 million should have been scored against the $17,500-per-candidate contribution limit.

Candidates also benefit from their party's national advertising campaigns and from advice on everything from how to organize a campaign to positions on issues.

Candidate's Own Money

Another source of money for campaigns is the candidate's own bank account. A candidate can reach as deeply into his own pocket as he wants because there are no limits on how much a candidate may contribute or loan to his own campaign. Deep personal pockets are not only welcomed by the parties but are sometimes even expected. According to political scientists David Magleby and Candice Nelson, the political parties may expect challengers and open-seat candidates to give or loan their campaigns $25,000 or more in House races and even more for Senate campaigns.[16]

In 1974 Congress attempted to set limits on how much House and Senate candidates could contribute to their own campaigns, but before the limits could take effect they were ruled unconstitutional by the Supreme Court in the 1976 *Buckley* decision. The Court ruled that "the candidate, no less than any other person, has a First Amendment right to engage in the discussion of public issues and vigorously and tirelessly to advocate his own election."

In keeping with the law's intent to clean up campaign finance activities, the justices also wrote that "the use of personal funds reduces the candidate's dependence on outside contributions and thereby counteracts the coercive pressure and attendant risks of abuse to which the act's contribution limitations are directed."

Most political observers agreed that the Court

had given wealthy contenders a tremendous advantage. Simply having access to money and a willingness to pour a lot of it into a campaign does not guarantee victory in November—or even in a primary. But wealthy candidates are able to afford expensive, professional consultants and plan their strategy with greater assurance than candidates without a personal fortune.

And money enables the wealthy, but unknown, candidate to make the first splash in a crowded field of relatively obscure contenders. Often the races that attract wealthy candidates are for open seats where there is no ordained successor. While dozens of potential candidates may jockey for position, the one who can begin a campaign with an early television blitz is likely to start several lengths ahead.

Television stations require campaigns to pay their bills before any material is aired. For this reason, the candidate who has the ability to loan or contribute a sizable sum can purchase expensive television advertising whenever he wants. Those who are less well-off financially are forced to wait until the money comes in before beginning their media buy.

As the campaign progresses, especially after the primary, the advantage of personal wealth diminishes. Candidates without a personal fortune then have greater access to other sources of money, particularly from party coffers; the field is smaller, making it easier for voters to draw clear distinctions between the candidates; and more free publicity is available as the general election draws nearer. There are many cases where a rich candidate was able to clear out the primary field but then lost in the general election.

While being able to bankroll a large portion of one's own campaign has many advantages, it also has several clear disadvantages. The most obvious and frequently encountered is that it opens the self-financed candidate to charges that he is trying to "buy" the election. Sometimes the opposition levels

the charge; often the media raise it.

Another disadvantage is that outside money is harder to raise. Potential contributors often assume the rich candidates do not need their money. In some cases that may be true. But from a political standpoint a healthy list of contributors can give a campaign more credibility by indicating that the candidate, besides having a fat war chest, has a broad base of support.

FEC figures for the 1989-90 election cycle showed that congressional candidates contributed $7 million to their own campaigns—$2.4 million in the Senate and $4.6 million in the House. Candidates loaned themselves an additional $30.9 million—nearly $10 million in the Senate and $21 million in the House. The largest user of personal money in the 1990 elections was James Rappaport, who loaned his Senate campaign $4.2 million but still lost to incumbent John Kerry, D-Mass.

As of 1991 the record high for personal expenditures—at least for the years in which these data were reported and disclosed by the FEC—had been set in 1984 by John D. Rockefeller IV, who loaned $10.3 million to his successful Senate campaign in West Virginia. By mid-1991 Rockefeller still hadn't paid himself back.

CAMPAIGN EXPENDITURES

Congressional candidates spent approximately $445 million in the 1989-90 election cycle. That amounted to a 3 percent decline from the $459 million spent in the 1987-88 election cycle and was the first time spending fell from one election cycle to the next since the FEC record keeping began in the 1970s. A slate of Senate contests marked by a lack of competition accounted for all of the decline.

House and Senate incumbents together spent a total of $276.5 million, while challengers spent $101 million and open-seat candidates, $67 million. Incumbents ended the campaign with a $95

Expenditures in Competitive 1988 Races

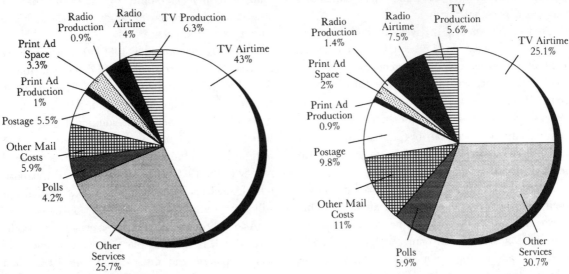

Senate Expenditures for Campaign Services

- Radio Production 0.9%
- Radio Airtime 4%
- TV Production 6.3%
- TV Airtime 43%
- Print Ad Space 3.3%
- Print Ad Production 1%
- Postage 5.5%
- Other Mail Costs 5.9%
- Polls 4.2%
- Other Services 25.7%

House Expenditures for Campaign Services

- Radio Production 1.4%
- Radio Airtime 7.5%
- TV Production 5.6%
- TV Airtime 25.1%
- Print Ad Space 2%
- Print Ad Production 0.9%
- Postage 9.8%
- Other Mail Costs 11%
- Polls 5.9%
- Other Services 30.7%

Source: **Based** on survey by Joseph E. Cantor and Kevin J. Coleman, *Summary Data on 1988 Congressional Candidates' Expenditure Survey,* Addendum to CRS Report No. 90-457 GOV, Report No. 90-526 GOV, Congressional Research Service, Library of Congress, November 8, 1990.

million cash surplus—proof that they had plenty of firepower to summon had they felt the need.

Figures for the Senate showed total expenditures of $180 million. Incumbents spent $113.5 million; challengers, $54.6 million; and open-seat candidates, $12 million. House candidates spent $265 million, with incumbents spending $163 million; challengers, $46.7 million; and open-seat candidates, $55 million.

How money is spent varies from one campaign to another. The needs of a House candidate are different from those of a Senate candidate. The needs of a challenger are different from those of an incumbent. A Senate candidate in a large state runs a different campaign from a candidate in a small

state. Representatives of urban, suburban, and rural congressional districts run vastly different campaigns. Costs skyrocket in hotly contested races and are negligible in races with little or no opposition.

But some generalizations may be made. Campaigns have to pay for staff and rent. They hire consultants, media experts, and polling firms. They send out computerized mailings. They buy postage, buttons, bumper stickers, billboards, newspaper ads, radio time, and television—lots of television.

Television Costs

Television advertising plays a major role in Senate campaigns. Being on or off the air wins elections.

"The hard fact of life for a candidate is that if you are not on TV, you are not truly in the race," Sen. Ernest F. Hollings, D-S.C., told a congressional committee in 1990.[17]

Moreover, on average, television is the single most expensive item in Senate candidates' campaign budgets. "You simply transfer money from contributors to television stations," as New Jersey Democrat Bill Bradley put it.[18]

The Congressional Research Service, in a survey of closely contested 1988 Senate campaigns, found that TV airtime accounted for 43 percent of campaign costs. All advertising costs—TV, radio, and print, along with their production costs—amounted to 58.5 percent of the expenditures.[19]

Television also has been an important tool in House campaigns but not as consistently so. In urban centers such as Los Angeles, New York, and Chicago, it has not been cost-effective, as an assistant to Rep. Howard L. Berman, D-Calif., who represented the San Fernando Valley suburbs of Los Angeles, explained:

> You spend thousands for one thirty-second spot on one TV station, in a city where cable is rampant and there are a zillion channels. There are sixteen to seventeen congressional districts in L.A., so the vast majority of those who see it are not your constituents and can't vote for you anyway.[20]

The CRS survey estimated spending by competitive House campaigns on television airtime at 25 percent of their campaign budgets. If all other advertising costs were added in, the percentage rose to 42.5 percent.

A study by the *Los Angeles Times* went beyond the closely contested races and researched all major party congressional candidates in the 1990 general election. It concluded that the amount of money Senate campaigns spent on television advertising had been overstated in debate on this issue, with some estimates as high as 50 to 75 percent. The survey pegged the cost of all advertising—television, radio, newspapers, and billboards, as well as media consultants—at 35 percent of Senate candidates' total expenditures and 25 percent for House candidates.[21]

Other Costs

The CRS survey found that the Senate campaigns spent 11.4 percent for postage and related costs, 4.2 percent for polling, and 25.7 percent for "other services," a catchall category that included overhead and related expenses. In the House races surveyed, 20.8 percent of their expenditures went for postage and related costs, 5.9 percent for polling, and 30.7 percent for other services.

The *Los Angeles Times* study found that Senate campaign expenditures included 25 percent for overhead, 24 percent for fund raising and direct mail, 7 percent for voter activity, and 5 percent for consultants and polls. House campaigns spent 27 percent for overhead, 16 percent for fund raising and direct mail, 13 percent for voter activity, and 8 percent for consultants and polls.

NOTES

1. House Democratic Study Group, "Growing Dependence on Big Contributors," Special Report No. 101-33 (July 30, 1990), 3-4.

2. "PAC Activity Falls in 1990 Elections," Federal Election Commission press release, March 31, 1991.

3. Norman J. Ornstein, Thomas E. Mann, and Michael J. Malbin, *Vital Statistics on Congress, 1989-1990* (Washington, D.C.: Congressional Quarterly, 1990), 85-86.

4. Frank J. Sorauf, *Money in American Elections* (Glenview, Ill.: Scott, Foresman, 1988), 73-74.

5. Larry J. Sabato, *Paying for Elections: The Campaign Finance Thicket* (New York: Twentieth Century Fund/Priority Press, 1989), 4.

6. Senate Committee on Rules and Administration, Hearings on Campaign Finance Reform, 101st Cong., 1st sess., Fred Wertheimer testimony, April 20, 1989, committee handout, 30.

7. Rinn-Sup Shinn, "Campaign Financing: National Public Opinion Polls," Report No. 91-346 GOV, Congressional Research Service, Library of Congress, April 12, 1991, i.

8. Quoted in Chuck Alston, "A Political Money Tree Waits for Incumbents in Need," *Congressional Quarterly Weekly Report,* June 30, 1990, 2026.

9. Quoted in Jeremy Gaunt, "Senate Freshmen Rewarded by Post-Election PAC Giving," *Congressional Quarterly Weekly Report,* September 5, 1987, 2134.

10. Herbert E. Alexander and Monica Bauer, *Financing the 1988 Election* (Boulder, Colo.: Westview Press, 1991), 69.

11. Ornstein, Mann, and Malbin, *Vital Statistics on Congress, 1989-1990,* 70.

12. Sorauf, *Money in American Elections,* 174.

13. Larry Makinson, *Open Secrets: The Dollar Power of PACs in Congress* (Washington, D.C.: Center for Responsive Politics (Congressional Quarterly, 1990), 77; Makinson, *PACs in Profile: Industry and Interest Group Spending in the 1990 Elections* (Washington,

D.C.: Center for Responsive Politics, May 2, 1991), 30.

14. Alexander and Bauer, *Financing the 1988 Election,* 76.

15. Joshua Goldstein, *The Fat Cats' Laundromat: Soft Money and the National Parties 1989-1990* (Center for Responsive Politics, May 1991), 1.

16. David B. Magleby and Candice J. Nelson, *The Money Chase: Congressional Campaign Finance Reform* (Washington, D.C.: Brookings Institution, 1990), 58.

17. Senate Committee on the Judiciary, Subcommittee on the Constitution, "Hearing on Campaign Finance Reform," 101st Cong., 2nd sess., February 28, 1990, 7.

18. Quoted in Chuck Alston, "Forcing Down Cost of TV Ads Appeals to Both Parties," *Congressional Quarterly Weekly Report,* March 16, 1991, 647.

19. Joseph E. Cantor and Kevin J. Coleman, "Summary Data on 1988 Congressional Candidates' Expenditure Survey," Addendum to CRS Report 90-457 GOV, Report No. 90-526 GOV, Congressional Research Service, Library of Congress, November 8, 1990, 5.

20. Quoted in Alston, "Forcing Down Cost of TV Ads Appeals to Both Parties," 648.

21. Sara Fritz and Dwight Morris, "Burden of TV Election Ads Exaggerated, Study Finds," *Los Angeles Times,* March 18, 1991, 1, 14-15.

CHAPTER 3

Campaign Finance:

Problems and Proposals

Congressional views both on problems in the system for financing elections and on possible remedies have been widely divergent. Debates over the system in the late 1980s and early 1990s revealed just how wide those gaps were and how difficult they would be to bridge.

Party was the key factor, as Democrats and Republicans took opposing views on issue after issue, with many votes routinely dividing along partisan lines. Chamber was also a significant factor, as House and Senate members headed off in different directions in their attempts at campaign finance reform.

PROBLEMS WITH THE SYSTEM

In the early 1990s there were three problems most frequently associated with the campaign finance system. One was the high cost of campaigning. That, in turn, led to another problem: the incessant search for contributions to pay the bills—a problem that had both personal and institutional ramifications. A third issue that was often raised was the inability of challengers to mount credible campaigns.

Campaigns' High Costs

"Politics has got so expensive that it takes lots of money to even get beat with," humorist Will Rogers remarked in 1931.[1] If it was true then, it was much more so by 1990.

The $445 million congressional candidates spent during the 1989-90 election cycle was less than the $459 million spent in the previous election. But it was a great deal more than the $194.8 million spent in 1977-78.

Senate Costs. A study by Common Cause, based on a six-year Senate election cycle, found that the twenty-eight Senate incumbents who had challengers in 1990 (four incumbents ran unopposed) spent an average of nearly $4.5 million each for their campaigns, while their challengers spent about $1.7 million each. All thirty-five winners in 1990—thirty-one incumbents, one challenger, and three open-seat candidates—spent an average of $3.7 million for their campaigns, twice the average $1.8 million spent by Senate losers, according to the study.[2]

The nearly $17.3 million incumbent Sen. Jesse Helms, R-N.C., spent during the six-year cycle

Campaign Spending by Election Year

(in millions of dollars)

Source: **Federal Election Commission.**

times more than losers—$371,846 to $134,200, according to the study. Nine House candidates—seven winners and two losers—spent more than $1 million each for their campaigns. Forty-seven candidates spent more than $750,000.

Why So Costly?   Several factors account for the spiraling costs of congressional campaigns. The most obvious cause has been inflation. As the costs of other goods and services in the economy inflated, so too did those of campaigns. A CRS study of Senate major party candidates who were on the general election ballot (primary losers were excluded) found that their total expenditures had risen from $73 million in 1980 to $172 million in 1990. But, taking inflation into account, these figures in constant 1982 dollars were $85 million in 1980 and $135 million in 1990.[4] A separate CRS study of House major party candidates found that their campaign costs had risen from $115.5 million in 1980 to $222.3 million in 1988, or, in constant 1982 dollars, from $134.8 million in 1980 to $181.6 million in 1988.[5]

But even when inflation is accounted for, the cost of campaigns has increased dramatically in recent decades, as the costs of fund raising and of educating the electorate have risen.

Since the 1960s congressional campaigns have undergone tremendous change. Most have been transformed from the volunteers-stuffing-envelopes-and-canvassing-voters type of campaign to highly technical, mechanized campaigns that are likely to use computerized mass mailings to solicit contributions and thirty-second TV ads to get their message across to voters. Candidates hire political consultants to direct their campaigns and polling companies to tell them how they are doing. All of the high-tech trappings of modern campaigns cost money—big money.

Population growth affects campaigns—as the electorate expands so too does the cost of reaching voters. Individual campaigns' costs are also affected

was the most spent by any Senate candidate on record at that time, according to Common Cause. Helms's opponent, Democrat Harvey Gantt, spent $7.7 million, bringing the total for that race to nearly $25 million. Helms's spending was a major factor in driving up the expenditure averages of the 1990 races. Even so, fourteen Senate candidates spent more than $4 million each.

House Costs.   A Common Cause study found that more than 90 percent of House incumbents who sought reelection in 1990 were either unopposed, financially unopposed, or in financially noncompetitive races.[3]

House winners on average spent nearly three

by the demographics of districts. Candidates in urban, suburban, or rural districts run very different campaigns with very different price tags. TV ads may not be cost-effective in an urban district, but they may be the only way a rural candidate can reach far-flung constituents.

The level of competition in a campaign also drives up the price of a campaign. Costs stay down if an incumbent has little or no opposition, but they rise sharply if an electoral threat appears. Candidates for open seats tend to raise and spend the most money, political scientist Gary Jacobson observed, "because when neither candidate enjoys the benefits of incumbency, both parties normally field strong candidates, and the election is usually close." Senate races also tend to attract money, according to Jacobson, because incumbent senators are often

perceived as vulnerable, most of their challengers are well-known public figures, and elections to the one hundred-member Senate have a greater political impact than do those to the 435-member House.[6]

Some observers believe that so much money is raised in campaigns because so much money is available. But incumbents have reasons to raise as much money as they can. One of these is "deterrence." They want to use their campaign war chests to scare off potential opponents. And if deterrence does not work, they want to be ready for any surprises their opponents may come up with.

Incumbents also feel more secure with sizable reserves in case a formidable challenger surfaces in some future race. That was particularly true in the late 1980s and early 1990s as some members

R. Michael Jenkins

Media consultant Peter Fenn advises Democratic candidates. Television advertising is the single most expensive item in many Senate campaign budgets.

anticipated tough challenges in 1992 because of redistricting. Others stockpile money in case they decide to run for higher office, such as a House member running for the Senate or a senator running for the presidency.

Quest for Money

By many accounts, one of the most onerous tasks a legislator faces is fund raising. Sorauf described it:

> To be sure, fund-raising takes a toll of the time, energy, and attention of legislators. The raising of money for the next campaign follows hard on the heels of the previous one, and there is little relief or surcease. It is a task that tires even the most enthusiastic fund-raisers, and it depresses those incumbents who find it distasteful.[7]

Facing reelection contests every two years, members of the House are essentially campaigning and fund raising all the time. One election campaign runs into the next. And even in the Senate, where the six-year term was once considered a luxury, members are beginning their campaigns earlier and earlier. The multimillion dollar price tags on some races require increasing attention to fund raising. During a 1987 debate on campaign finance legislation, reform advocate Sen. David L. Boren, D-Okla., told the Senate: "We have people . . . who come to this body and have their first fundraisers in this town before they ever cast their first votes as members of the House or Senate." [8] Makinson found that for a senator to raise the $4 million that the average winning Senate race cost in 1988, he or she would have had to raise nearly $13,000 every week during the entire six-year term.[9] Few, if any, senators actually did that, but it illustrated the magnitude of the task.

More than a few find the task demeaning. At one Democratic party training session, candidates were offered the following advice: "Learn how to beg, and do it in a way that leaves you some dignity." [10] That may be easier said than done, as Sen. Tom Daschle, D-S.D., found during his successful 1986 campaign to unseat an incumbent senator: "You're with people you have nothing in common with. You have a cosmetic conversation. You paint the best face you can on their issues and feel uncomfortable through the whole thing. You sheepishly accept their check and leave feeling not very good." [11]

At least he left with the check, which is more than can be said for many challengers. Attempting to unseat a sitting member of Congress is an enormously difficult task for a number of reasons, not the least of which is the obstacle of having to bankroll a campaign. Rep. David E. Price, D-N.C., a political scientist who ran successfully against an incumbent in 1986, said that he had undertaken few ventures as difficult and discouraging as raising money for his primary campaign. He held small fund raisers, sent mail appeals to party activists, and approached potential large contributors, with mixed success. He and his wife contacted people on their old Christmas card lists, as well as professional colleagues and family members. They took out a second mortgage on their home. Price won the primary but still found fund raising for the general election a continuing struggle. He later reflected on his campaign:

> I will . . . never forget how difficult it was to raise the first dollars. I understand quite well why many potentially strong challengers and potentially able representatives simply cannot or will not do what it takes to establish financial "viability" and why so many who do reach that point can do so only on the basis of personal wealth. The modus operandi of most large contributors, PACs, and even party committees often makes their

calculations of an incumbent's "safety" a self-fulfilling prophecy.[12]

The difficulties that surround fund raising have institutional, as well as personal, repercussions. For one thing, the time members spend raising money is time away from the business of legislating. Sen. Robert Byrd said that one of his biggest problems as Senate majority leader was accommodating the senators' need for time away from the floor to raise money for their campaigns. Testifying before the Senate Rules Committee in 1987, Byrd painted a picture of a Senate colored by money, a Senate increasingly attuned to the fat cats and special interests, a Senate in which members sought Mondays off and an early close to Friday business so they could jet off to places like New York, Miami, and Los Angeles. "They have to go raise the money and they don't want any roll-call votes," Byrd lamented. "Now how can a majority leader run the Senate under such circumstances?" To Byrd the culprit was clear: "Mad, seemingly limitless escalation of campaign costs."[13] Byrd ended up revamping the Senate's work schedule in 1988 to give members time off to campaign and attend fund raisers.

As Rep. Price indicated, there is another institutional consequence: the high cost of elections discourages people from running for Congress. "Potential challengers or candidates for open seats realize that unless they can raise a lot of money, they have little chance of winning," wrote Magleby and Nelson. As a result, party committees have found "it is increasingly hard to convince people to run, given the low probability of success and the high investment of time and money necessary to even hope to be competitive."[14]

Incumbent Advantage

Voters in 1990 returned congressional incumbents to Washington en masse, as they pretty much had been doing for years.

Of the 406 House incumbents who ran in the general election in 1990, 391 won—a 96 percent reelection rate. The last time the reelection rate in the House had dipped below 90 percent was in 1974. On the Senate side the reelection rates have been much more erratic. But in the 1990 election thirty-one of thirty-two incumbents seeking reelection won, which put the reelection rate at 96.9 percent. *(Box, p. 24)*

This very decided advantage of incumbents at the polls has produced much study and speculation. According to Roger H. Davidson and Walter J. Oleszek, political scientists have launched "a vertible cottage industry" to answer the question of why incumbents are so formidable.[15]

Several reasons can be cited. Incumbents have name recognition. They have a public record to run on, which can be especially helpful if they can demonstrate they have voted to protect the interests of their constituents and have brought home federal grants and projects. Incumbents are highly visible because of easy and regular access to the media. Moreover, they enjoy a number of perquisites, the most important being large staffs on Capitol Hill and in state or district offices ready to respond to the needs and inquiries of constituents. Thanks to the franking privilege, most letters and newsletters to constituents can be mailed free of charge. Members also benefit from allowances for phone calls and for travel back to their home district or state.

Incumbents also enjoy a distinct advantage in raising money for their reelection campaigns. FEC figures showed that Senate incumbents in the 1989-90 election cycle raised almost $119 million, while challengers raised about $55 million. Moreover, incumbent senators clearly had more to spend in 1990 had they needed it. Four senators each finished with more than $1 million in the bank.

House incumbents widened their fund-raising advantage over challengers to nearly four to one in 1989-90. Incumbents raised $181 million, compared with $47.5 million raised by challengers.

Incumbent Reelection Rates, 1960-1990

Year/office	Number of incumbents			Percentage who won	Year/office	Number of incumbents			Percentage who won
	Ran	Won	Lost			Ran	Won	Lost	
1960					1976				
House	400	374	26	93.5	House	381	368	13	96.6
Senate	29	28	1	96.6	Senate	25	16	9	64.0
1962					1978				
House	396	381	15	94.3	House	378	359	19	95.0
Senate	34	29	5	85.3	Senate	22	15	7	68.1
1964					1980				
House	389	344	45	88.4	House	392	361	31	90.7
Senate	32	28	4	87.5	Senate	25	16	9	64.0
1966					1982				
House	402	362	40	90.1	House	381	352	29	92.4
Senate	29	28	1	96.6	Senate	30	28	2	93.3
1968					1984				
House	401	396	5	98.8	House	407	391	16	96.1
Senate	24	20	4	83.3	Senate	29	26	3	89.7
1970					1986				
House	391	379	12	96.9	House	391	385	6	98.5
Senate	29	23	6	79.3	Senate	28	21	7	75.0
1972					1988				
House	380	367	13	95.6	House	408	402	6	98.5
Senate	25	20	5	80.0	Senate	27	23	4	85.1
1974					1990				
House	383	343	40	89.6	House	406	391	15	96.3
Senate	25	23	2	92.0	Senate	32	31	1	96.9

Note: Includes general elections only.
Source: Congressional Quarterly records.

House incumbents also ended up with surpluses after the 1990 election—altogether, they had $77 million left over.

Both individual donors and PACs favored incumbents. Sixty-four percent of all individual contributions went to incumbents in the 1989-90 election cycle. The percentage was even higher for PAC contributions—77.5 percent went to incumbents. The overwhelming bias of PACs toward incumbents was a key issue in campaign finance debates of the late 1980s and early 1990s.

The implications of the tilt toward incumbents preoccupied members, reformers, and observers of Congress alike. Some warned of a trend toward a "permanent Congress" with little turnover, and they deplored special interests' buying access to members of Congress. But others dismissed the notion and framed these contributions in a more positive light—contributors wanted to go with a winner, and most incumbents were seen as sure bets.

That contributors favor incumbents was only too clear to Rep. Price during his campaign to unseat an incumbent. He wrote:

> Mainly, the organized groups and political action committees ... simply stayed out of the primary. Their general rule of thumb is to support an incumbent if he or she has been reasonably receptive to their concerns. Playing the percentages, it is reasonable for PACs to expect that the incumbent will survive and that they will need to deal with that member in the future. But even those issue-oriented Democratic-leaning PACs who had good reason to like me and to oppose the incumbent were usually unwilling to help me until I had survived the primary and could show that I had a good chance to win in November.[16]

PROPOSALS FOR CHANGE

Congressional leaders of both parties put campaign finance reform at the top of their agendas in the early 1990s, but whether they would be able to produce a blueprint for bridging their differences was an open question. Each party wanted to capitalize on its strong points and curb those of the other party.

The Democrats contended that the system operated like an arms race—that candidates engaged in a never-ending quest for a financial edge. Hence, they insisted that any new law had to limit campaign spending. Democrats also proposed public financing of congressional campaigns under certain circumstances.

Republicans, on the other hand, saw the problem as one of tainted sources of money. Instead of capping spending, they proposed curbing specific sources, such as PACS. Republicans at one time had favored PACs but had switched their position after PACs in the mid-1980s began to support House incumbents, without regard to party, and the majority of PAC contributions had shifted from the Republicans to the Democrats. The GOP also wanted to curb large out-of-state contributions. And they wanted to encourage political parties to spend even more money in behalf of their candidates. What Republicans feared most was that locking in spending levels might lock in a Democratic majority.

Further complicating matters was the fact that incumbent factions in each party savored the easy flow of money from Washington fund raisers. House Democrats in particular found it difficult to think of parting with PAC dollars. Even some Republicans were wary of overthrowing a system that kept them in office, albeit in the minority.

Contribution Restrictions

The question of what to do, if anything, about PACs was particularly divisive on Capitol Hill. The Senate in 1990 and again in 1991 passed reform legislation that included a ban on PACs. Some accused the Senate of posturing, knowing full well that House members, who received a much higher portion of their contributions from PACs than did senators, would vote to preserve PACs or that the Supreme Court ultimately would declare the ban unconstitutional.

Proposals to limit but not ban PACs generated another type of controversy. Although PACs could give $10,000 to a candidate in an election cycle ($5,000 for the primary and $5,000 for the general), most gave far less. However, labor PACs often gave Democrats in close races the full $10,000 permitted—money they did not want to lose.

There were also proposals regarding individual giving. One proposal was to allow donors to give more money to candidates from their own congressional district or state. Supporters said that a member ought to depend more on his own constituents for money than on anyone else. Opponents argued that federal legislators were everyone's business. Republicans advanced this cause, embraced to a limited extent by Senate Democrats.

Limiting PAC and individual contributions raised an important secondary issue: replacing the lost dollars. Any of the proposals would have left a gaping hole in many campaign treasuries. One potential substitute was public money—either direct grants or vouchers that could be used to purchase services such as television time or postage.

Estimates of how much public financing would cost depended on the specific plan, but the figures as of the early 1990s ran as high as $300 million per election cycle, if benefits were extended to every House and Senate candidate. Supporters contended that the cost was modest compared with the benefit of cleaning up campaigns. But opponents deplored the idea of a deficit-ridden government subsidizing congressional elections.

A voluntary tax checkoff system had been used since 1976 to provide public funds for presidential campaigns. But because the fund was going broke, due to dwindling contributions and inflation, many doubted that congressional campaigns could rely solely on a tax checkoff system.

Republicans offered political parties as an alternative source of funds. They proposed letting parties give more to, or spend more in behalf of, their candidates than existing law allowed. Democrats were not enthusiastic about this idea, primarily because the GOP was far better at raising money.

Finally, there was the issue of helping challengers, emphasized by those who saw the lack of competitive elections as one of democracy's chief ills. Proposals in this area—which included lifting contribution limits on part of the money raised by challengers or allowing parties to match a portion of the challengers' money—were of great interest to Republicans, who were driven in part by the desire to wrest majority status from the Democrats.

Campaign Spending

Another extremely divisive issue in the campaign funding debate was the proposal that a limit be set on campaign spending.

For one thing, the Supreme Court in 1976 had ruled that a mandatory limit was unconstitutional. That decision led to proposals designed to induce voluntary participation, such as providing candidates who agreed to abide by the limit with low-cost or free television and radio advertising, reduced postage costs, and direct grants.

And then there was the partisan aspect of the issue. Many Republicans believed, and most academic experts agreed, that spending limits favored incumbents because challengers had a greater need to spend money. Jacobson found that marginal returns on campaign spending were much greater for challengers than for incumbents. "The more challengers spend . . . the greater their share of the vote, and their level of spending has a substantially larger impact on their probability of winning elections than does the incumbents' level of spending," he wrote.[17] Jacobson's findings led to an obvious corollary: An arbitrary ceiling could prevent a challenger from spending enough money to win. Democrats, however, maintained that limits could be set that would level the field.

The intransigence of the party positions was illustrated by the comments of two leading figures in the Senate debate:

"One thing is clear: The only meaningful way to reform the Senate election finance system is to have limits on campaign spending," Majority Leader George J. Mitchell, D-Maine, said on the floor.

Sen. Mitch McConnell, R-Ky., staked out the opposing point of view in an interview: "There won't be a bill with spending limits or public financing.... That's a typical Democratic response: Hire a bunch of bureaucrats, get into the Treasury, and start a new government program." [18]

One issue that did unite senators on both sides of the aisle was cutting the cost of buying television time. But here again it was not as burning an issue in the House, where members were far less dependent on costly TV ads than senators were.

And so the heated debate over the financing of elections continued, as it had throughout the history of American politics.

NOTES

1. Quoted in Larry J. Sabato, *Paying for Elections: The Campaign Finance Thicket* (New York: Twentieth Century Fund/Priority Press, 1989), 11.

2. Common Cause News, press release of February 28, 1991, 5-7.

3. Common Cause News, press release of March 26, 1991, 3, 5, 9.

4. David C. Huckabee and Joseph E. Cantor, "Senate Campaign Expenditures, Receipts, and Sources of Funds: 1980-1990," Report No. 91-406 GOV, Congressional Research Service, Library of Congress, May 8, 1991, 2.

5. David C. Huckabee and Joseph E. Cantor, "House Campaign Expenditures: 1980-1988," Report No. 89-534 GOV, Congressional Research Service, Library of Congress, September 20, 1989, 2, 9.

6. Gary C. Jacobson, "Money in the 1980 and 1982 Congressional Elections," in *Money and Politics in the United States: Financing Elections in the 1980s,* ed. Michael J. Malbin (Washington, D.C.: American Enterprise Institute for Public Policy Research, 1984), 58.

7. Frank J. Sorauf, *Money in American Elections* (Glenview, Ill.: Scott, Foresman, 1988), 333.

8. *Congressional Record,* 100th Cong., 1st sess., June 3, 1987, S7540.

9. Larry Makinson, *The Price of Admission: An Illustrated Atlas of Campaign Spending in the 1988 Congressional Elections* (Washington, D.C.: Center for Responsive Politics, 1989), 23.

10. Diane Granat, "Parties' Schools for Politicians Grooming Troops for Elections," *Congressional Quarterly Weekly Report,* May 5, 1984, 1036.

11. Quoted in Andy Plattner, "The High Cost of Holding—and Keeping—Public Office," *U.S. News & World Report,* June 22, 1987, 30.

12. David E. Price, "The House of Representatives: A Report from the Field," in *Congress Reconsidered,* 4th ed., ed. Lawrence C. Dodd and Bruce I. Oppenheimer (Washington, D.C.: CQ Press, 1989), 417-418.

13. Senate Committee on Rules and Administration, *Hearings on Senate Campaign Finance Proposals,* 100th Cong., 1st sess., March 5 and 18, April 22 and 23, 1987, 7-8.

14. David B. Magleby and Candice J. Nelson, *The Money Chase: Congressional Campaign Finance Reform* (Washington, D.C.: Brookings Institution, 1990), 44.

15. Roger H. Davidson and Walter J. Oleszek, *Congress and Its Members,* 3rd ed. (Washington, D.C.: CQ Press, 1990), 61.

16. David E. Price, "The House of Representatives: A Report from the Field," in *Congress Reconsidered,* 4th ed., ed. Lawrence C. Dodd and Bruce I. Oppenheimer (Washington, D.C.: CQ Press, 1989), 415.

17. Gary C. Jacobson, "Parties and PACs in Congressional Elections," in *Congress Reconsidered,* 4th ed., ed. Lawrence C. Dodd and Bruce I. Oppenheimer (Washington, D.C.: CQ Press, 1989), 134.

18. Quoted in Chuck Alston, "Image Problems Propel Congress Back to Campaign Finance Bills," 281.

CHAPTER 4

Financing Campaigns:
Historical Development

In early American politics the source of money to finance a political campaign was never a question. Politics was a gentleman's pursuit and the gentleman was to pay. But, as political scientist Robert Mutch points out, the expenses were small and campaigns in the modern sense were few. "Candidates were supposed to attract support by virtue of their reputations, not by actually mingling with voters," Mutch wrote.[1] Candidates' expenses might have included the costs of printing and distributing campaign literature or perhaps providing food and drink for the voters on election day.

George Washington, for example, during his campaign for the House of Burgesses in Virginia in 1757, dispensed twenty-eight gallons of rum, fifty gallons of rum punch, thirty-four gallons of wine, forty-six gallons of beer, and two gallons of cider royal! "Even in those days this was considered a large campaign expenditure," writer George Thayer observed, "because there were only 391 voters in his district, for an average outlay of more than a quart and a half per person."[2]

By the early nineteenth century politics no longer was the exclusive domain of the wealthy merchant or the gentleman farmer. The professional politician had emerged. Lacking personal wealth, the new breed was dependent on others for campaign support and on salaries for their livelihood. Modern political parties also began to emerge, and with them came the spoils system. When a new president came in, government jobs were transferred to his supporters. It was not long before the new appointees were having to pay for the privilege of a government job, with the political parties exacting percentages from the salaries of federal employees.

The first known cases of assessments on government workers were levied by the Democratic party on U.S. customs employees in New York City during the 1830s. But attempts to legislate against the practice went nowhere because, as Mutch noted, "few politicians were willing to eliminate such a valuable source of party funds, and the system of assessments continued to grow."[3]

The first provision of federal law relating to campaign finance was incorporated into an act of March 2, 1867, making naval appropriations for fiscal 1868. The final section of the act read:

> And be it further enacted, That no officer or employee of the government shall require or request any workingman in any navy yard to contribute or pay any money for political

purposes, nor shall any workingman be removed or discharged for political opinion; and any officer or employee of the government who shall offend against the provisions of this section shall be dismissed from the service of the United States.

Reports circulated the following year that at least 75 percent of the money raised by the Republican Congressional Committee came from federal officeholders. Continuing agitation on this and other aspects of the spoils system in federal employment—tragically highlighted by the assassination in 1881 of President James A. Garfield by a disappointed office seeker—led to adoption of the 1883 Civil Service Reform Act. The act, also known as the Pendleton Act, authorized the establishment of personnel rules, one of which stated, "That no person in the public service is for that reason under any obligation to contribute to any political fund . . . and that he will not be removed or otherwise prejudiced for refusing to do so." The law made it a crime for any federal employee to solicit campaign funds from another federal employee.

But shrewd campaign managers found money elsewhere. Business money had become increasingly important in the post-Civil War period and was dominant by the close of the century. In the legendary 1896 campaign between Republican William McKinley and Democrat-Populist William Jennings Bryan, McKinley's successful effort was managed by Marcus A. (Mark) Hanna, a wealthy Ohio financier and industrialist who turned the art of political fund raising into a system for assessing campaign contributions from banks and corporations.

As these political contributions grew, so too did public concern over the role of corporate money in politics. "The concern among the electorates of the industrialized nineteenth century was that their elected representatives might not be the real policymakers, that government might still be controlled

Links between money and politics were a target for editorial cartoonists even before Thomas Nast drew this in 1871.

by those who provided campaign funds," Mutch wrote.[4] In the late 1800s several states enacted campaign finance laws, some requiring disclosure of information on the sources and uses of campaign contributions and others actually prohibiting corporate contributions. The push was on for action on the national level.

EARLY LEGISLATION

Reacting to the increasingly lavish corporate involvement in political campaigns, the hearty band of reformers known as the "muckrakers" pressed for the nation's first extensive campaign finance legislation. During the first decade of the twentieth century, they worked to expose big business's influence on government through unrestrained spending on behalf of favored candidates.

Corporate Contribution Ban

Revelations during congressional hearings that several corporations had secretly financed Theodore Roosevelt's 1904 presidential campaign provided impetus for change. The establishment of the National Publicity Law Organization, headed by former Rep. Perry Belmont, D-N.Y., focused further attention on the issue. President Roosevelt, in his annual message to Congress, proposed on December 5, 1905, that "all contributions by corporations to any political committee or for any political purpose should be forbidden by law." Roosevelt repeated the proposal the following December, suggesting that it be the first item of congressional business. And in his December 1907 message, Roosevelt joined those calling for the "very radical measure" of public funding of elections.

In response Congress in 1907 passed the first federal campaign finance law, the Tillman Act, which made it unlawful for a corporation or a national bank to make "a money contribution in connection with any election" of candidates for federal office. Although Roosevelt is generally regarded as having initiated the series of actions leading to the 1907 law, Mutch points out that the bill passed by Congress had actually been written and introduced five years earlier.[5]

Disclosure Mandated

Three years later the first Federal Corrupt Practices Act was passed, establishing disclosure requirements for U.S. House candidates. Specifically, the 1910 law required every political committee "which shall in two or more states influence the result or attempt to influence the result of an election at which Representatives in Congress are to be elected" to file with the clerk of the House of Representatives, within thirty days after the election, the name and address of each contributor of $100 or more, the name and address of each

recipient of $10 or more from the committee, and the total amounts that the committee received and disbursed. Individuals who engaged in similar activities outside the framework of committees also were required to submit such reports.

The following year, legislation was passed extending the filing requirements to committees influencing senatorial elections and requiring candidates for House and Senate seats to file financial reports. (Popular election of senators, in place of election by state legislatures, was mandated by the Seventeenth Amendment, approved by Congress in 1912 and ratified in 1913.) The most important innovation of the 1911 act was the placing of a limitation on the amount a candidate could spend toward his nomination and election: a candidate for the Senate, no more than $10,000 or the maximum amount permitted in his state, whichever was less; for the House, no more than $5,000 or the maximum amount permitted in his state, whichever was less.

1925 Corrupt Practices Act

No further changes in federal campaign law were made for more than a decade. But then the system was overhauled with passage of the Federal Corrupt Practices Act of 1925, which served as the basic campaign finance law until 1971.

The Teapot Dome scandal gave Congress the push it needed to pass reform legislation. During a congressional investigation of alleged improprieties in the Harding administration's leasing of naval oil reserves to private operators, it had been discovered that an official of the company that had leased the Teapot Dome reserve in Wyoming had not only bribed the official in charge of the leasing but had also contributed generously to the Republican party to help retire its 1920 campaign debt. The contribution had been made in a nonelection year and therefore did not have to be reported under existing law—a loophole that was closed by the 1925 act's requirement that contributions be reported, whether made in an election year or not.

The 1925 act regulated campaign spending and disclosure of receipts and expenditures by House and Senate candidates, as well as disclosure by national political committees and their subsidiaries and by other committees seeking to influence elections in more than one state. The 1925 act limited its restrictions to general election campaigns, because at the time it was unsettled whether Congress had the power to regulate primary elections.

The act revised the amounts that candidates could legally spend. Unless a state law prescribed a smaller amount, the act set the ceilings at $10,000 for a Senate candidate and $2,500 for a House candidate; or an amount equal to three cents for each vote cast in the last preceding election for the office sought, but not more than $25,000 for the Senate and $5,000 for the House.

The 1925 act incorporated the existing prohibition against campaign contributions by corporations and national banks, the ban on solicitation of political contributions from federal employees by candidates or other federal employees, and the requirement that reports on campaign finances be filed. It prohibited giving or offering money to anyone in exchange for his vote. In amending the provisions of the 1907 act on contributions, the new law substituted for the word "money" the phrase "a gift, subscription, loan, advance, or deposit of money, or anything of value."

The Corrupt Practices Act, however, was riddled with loopholes, making reported amounts merely indicative and by no means complete. The act contained no provisions for enforcement. It did not mandate publication of the reports or review of the reports for errors and omissions. It did not require reports of contributions and expenditures in either presidential or congressional primary campaigns, nor in connection with a party's presidential nomination. It did not require reports by political committees so long as they confined their activities to a single state and were not actual subsidiaries of a national political committee. Frequently, congressional candidates reported they had received and spent nothing on their campaigns, maintaining that the campaign committees established to elect them to office had been working without their "knowledge and consent."

Candidates were able to evade the spending limitations by channeling most of their campaign expenditures through separate committees that were not required to report federally, thus making the federal ceilings, from a practical standpoint, meaningless.

No candidate for the House or the Senate ever was prosecuted under the 1925 act, although it was widely known that most candidates spent more than the act allowed and did not report all they spent. Only two persons elected to Congress—two senators-elect in 1927—ever were excluded for spending in excess of the act's limits.

In 1934 a case reached the Supreme Court that required the Court to rule on the constitutionality of the 1925 act's requirement that political committees seeking to influence the election of presidential electors in two or more states file contribution and spending reports. In its decision in *Burroughs and Cannon v. United States* (290 U.S. 534), the Court on January 8, 1934, upheld the act's applicability to the election of presidential electors and implicitly sanctioned federal regulation of campaign financing in congressional elections.

On the topic of disclosure, the Court stated: "Congress reached the conclusion that public disclosure of political contributions, together with the names of contributors and other details, would tend to prevent the corrupt use of money to affect elections. The verity of this conclusion reasonably cannot be denied."

Hatch Act and Labor Restrictions

During the period between the early efforts to regulate spending and the broad reforms of the

1970s, some laws related to campaign financing were enacted, although they had less direct effects than the corrupt practices laws.

A 1939 law, commonly called the Hatch Act but also known as the Clean Politics Act, barred federal employees from active participation in national politics and prohibited collection of political contributions from persons receiving relief funds provided by the federal government.

In 1940 an amendment to the Hatch Act made three significant additions to campaign finance law. First, it forbade federal contractors, whether individuals or companies, to contribute to any political committee or candidate. Second, it asserted Congress's right to regulate primary elections for the nomination of candidates for federal office and made it unlawful for anyone to contribute more than $5,000 to a federal candidate or political committee in a single year. But Congress opened a big loophole when it specifically exempted from this limitation "contributions made to or by a state or local committee."

And third, the 1940 amendment placed a ceiling of $3 million in a calendar year on expenditures by a political committee operating in two or more states. In practice, however, the parties easily evaded this stipulation.

Three years later Congress passed the War Labor Disputes Act (Smith-Connally Act), temporarily extending the 1907 prohibition on political contributions by national banks and corporations to include labor unions. This prohibition was made permanent by the Labor-Management Relations Act of 1947 (Taft-Hartley Act).

Restrictions on Primaries Upheld

Legislative and judicial decisions in the first half of the twentieth century repeatedly redefined the relationship of campaign finance laws to primary elections. The 1911 act limiting campaign expenditures in congressional elections covered primaries

as well as general elections. In 1921, however, the Supreme Court in the case of *Newberry v. United States* (256 U.S. 232) struck down the law's application to primaries on the ground that the power the Constitution gave Congress to regulate the "manner of holding the election" did not extend to party primaries and conventions. The Corrupt Practices Act of 1925 exempted primaries from its coverage.

The Hatch Act amendments of 1940 made primaries again subject to federal restrictions on campaign contributions despite the *Newberry* decision. This legislation was upheld in 1941, when the Supreme Court in *United States v. Classic et al.* (313 U.S. 299) reversed its *Newberry* decision by ruling that Congress has the power to regulate primary elections when the primary is an integral part of the process of selecting candidates for federal office. The *Classic* decision was reaffirmed by the Court in 1944 in *Smith v. Allwright* (321 U.S. 649). When the Taft-Hartley Act was adopted in 1947, its prohibition of political contributions by corporations, national banks, and labor organizations was phrased to cover primaries as well as general elections.

LOOPHOLES ABOUND

Even with the revisions of the 1930s and 1940s, the campaign system was filled with loopholes. In a 1967 message to Congress proposing election reforms, President Lyndon B. Johnson said of the Corrupt Practices and Hatch acts: "Inadequate in their scope when enacted, they are now obsolete. More loophole than law, they invite evasion and circumvention."

Contributors' Loopholes

The Corrupt Practices Act required the treasurer of a political committee active in two or more states to report at specified times the name and address of every donor of $100 or more to a campaign. To evade such recording, a donor could give less than $100 to each of numerous committees supporting the candidate of his choice. A Senate subcommittee in 1956 checked the contributions of sums between $50 and $99.99 to one committee. It found that of ninety-seven contributions in that range, eighty-eight were over $99, including fifty-seven that were exactly $99.99.

Technically, an individual could not contribute more than $5,000 to any national committee or federal candidate. However, he could contribute unlimited funds to state, county, and local groups that passed along the money in the organization's name.

Members of the same family could legally contribute up to $5,000 each. A wealthy donor wanting to give more than $5,000 to a candidate or a political committee could privately subsidize gifts by his relatives. Each such subsidized gift could amount to $5,000. In this way, the donor could arrange for his brothers, sisters, uncles, aunts, wife, and children to make $5,000 gifts.

According to data from the Survey Research Center at the University of Michigan, only about 8 percent of the population contributed in 1968. Both parties relied on big contributors. In every presidential election in the 1950s and 1960s, with one exception, the Democratic National Committee relied on contributors of more than $500 for more than 60 percent of its funds. For the same period, again with the exception of one election year, the Republican National Committee received more than 50 percent of its contributions from donations of more than $500.

Each party could count on support from certain wealthy contributors. Among the Republicans were the Mellons, Rockefellers, and Whitneys. Among the Democrats were the Laskers, Kennedys, and Harrimans. Large contributions also came from foreigners.

Corporations. Corporations could skirt the prohibition of contributions to a political campaign by giving bonuses or salary increases to executives in the expectation that as individuals they would make corresponding political contributions to candidates favored by the corporation.

Political campaign managers learned to watch for contribution checks drawn directly on corporate funds and to return them to avoid direct violation of the law. Often this money made its way back to the political managers in some other form.

Corporations were allowed to place advertisements in political journals, even though there was no apparent benefit to the corporations from the ads, and they could lend billboards, office furniture, equipment, mailing lists, and airplanes to candidates or political committees. If a loan of this kind was deemed a violation of the letter of the law, the corporation could rent these items to a candidate or committee, instead of lending them, and then write off the rental fee as uncollectible.

Unions. Labor unions could contribute to a candidate or political committee funds collected from members apart from dues. Money could be taken directly from union treasuries and used for technically "nonpartisan" purposes, such as promoting voter registration, encouraging members to vote, or publishing the voting records of members of Congress or state legislators.

Organized labor's registration and get-out-the-vote drives overwhelmingly supported Democratic candidates, being keyed to areas where regular Democratic efforts were considered deficient or where an overwhelming Democratic vote was traditionally necessary to overcome a Republican plurality in some other section of the district, state, or country.

Public service activities, such as union newspapers or radio programs, could be financed directly from regular union treasuries. As with corporate newspapers and radio programs, a sharply partisan viewpoint could be, and often was, expressed.

Candidates' Loopholes

Federal or state limitations on the amount of money a candidate might knowingly receive or spend were easily evaded. A loophole in the law enabled numerous candidates to report that they received and spent not one cent on their campaigns because any financial activity was conducted without their "knowledge or consent." In 1964 four senators reported that their campaign books showed zero receipts and zero expenditures— Vance Hartke, D-Ind.; Roman L. Hruska, R-Neb.; Edmund S. Muskie, D-Maine; and John C. Stennis, D-Miss.

Four years later, when Sen. George McGovern, D-S.D., reported no receipts or expenditures, one of his staff explained that they were careful to make sure that McGovern never saw the campaign receipts. Two senators elected in 1968—William B. Saxbe, R-Ohio, and Richard S. Schweiker, R-Pa.—reported general election expenditures of $769,614 and $664,614, respectively, to their state authorities, but expenditures of only $20,962 and $5,736, respectively, to the secretary of the Senate.

Another measure of the recorded figures' incompleteness was the contrast between the reported total political spending in 1960—$28,326,322— and the $175 million spending estimate by political experts. In 1962, $18,404,115 was reported spent in congressional races, but Congressional Quarterly estimated the actual total at almost $100 million.

The credibility gap fostered by the "knowledge or consent" loophole was widened further because the Federal Corrupt Practices Act applied only to political committees operating in two or more states. If a committee operated in one state only and was not a subdivision of a national committee, the law did not apply. If a committee operated in the District of Columbia only, receiving funds there and mailing checks to candidates in a single state, the law did not cover it.

Limits on the expenditures that a political committee might make were evaded by establishing more than one committee and apportioning receipts and expenditures among them, so that no one committee exceeded the limit. Because the law limited annual spending by a political committee operating in two or more states to $3 million annually, the major parties formed committees under various names, each of which was free to spend up to $3 million.

Although the Corrupt Practices Act provided criminal penalties for false reporting or failure to report, successive administrations ignored them, even though news reporters repeatedly uncovered violations. Eisenhower administration Attorney General Herbert Brownell stated in 1954 the Justice Department's position that the initiative in such cases rested with the secretary of the Senate and the clerk of the House, and that policy was continued.

Secretaries of the Senate and clerks of the House for many years winked at violations of the filing requirements. The situation changed in 1967 when former Rep. W. Pat Jennings, D-Va., became House clerk. He began sending lists of violations to the Justice Department for prosecution, but then the department refused to act.

Attempts at Reform

Attempts to rewrite the 1925 act were made regularly during the late 1950s and 1960s but with little success.

In April 1962 the President's Commission on Campaign Costs issued a report recommending proposals to encourage greater citizen participation in financing presidential campaigns. The commission had been named in October 1961 by President John F. Kennedy. Alexander Heard, then dean of the University of North Carolina Graduate School, was the chairman and Herbert Alexander was the executive director. Among the commission's recommendations were that:

- Tax credits or deductions be given for certain levels of individuals' political contributions.
- The existing limits on expenditures of interstate political committees and individual contributions to those committees be repealed, leaving no limit.
- All candidates for president and vice president and committees spending at least $2,500 a year be required to report expenditures made in both primary and general election campaigns.
- A Registry of Election Finance be established to help enforce political financing regulations.
- The government pay the transition costs of a president-elect during the period between election and inauguration.

In May 1962 President Kennedy submitted to Congress five draft bills encompassing proposals identical or similar to the commission's. But the only bill reported was one to finance transition costs, and it died on the House floor.

Tax Checkoff Attempt.
Congress did not act again in the area of campaign finance until the mid-1960s, when it passed a tax checkoff plan to provide government subsidies to presidential election campaigns. An act approved in 1966 authorized any individual paying federal income tax to direct that one dollar of the tax due in any year be paid into a Presidential Election Campaign Fund. The fund, to be set up in the U.S. Treasury, was to disburse its receipts proportionately among political parties whose presidential candidates had received 5 million or more votes in the preceding presidential election. Congress, however, failed to adopt the required guidelines for distribution of the funds, so the 1966 act was in effect voided in 1967.

Skyrocketing Costs.
But the mood in Washington was beginning to change. In addition to growing irritation with the toothlessness of the disclosure laws, uneasiness was increasing over campaign costs.

Rising campaign costs were evident soon after World War II. Heard wrote in 1960:

Radio and television broadcasting eat up millions. Thousands go to pay for rent, electricity, telephone, telegraph, auto hire, airplanes, airplane tickets, registration drives, hillybilly bands, public relations counsel, the Social Security tax on payrolls. Money pays for writers and for printing what they write, for advertising in many blatant forms, and for the boodle in many subtle guises. All these expenditures are interlarded with outlays for the hire of donkeys and elephants, for comic books, poll taxes and sample ballots, for gifts to the United Negro College Fund and the Police Relief Association, for a $5.25 traffic ticket in Maryland and $66.30 worth of "convention liquor" in St. Louis....[6]

Radio and television ads came to occupy a greater and greater portion of campaign budgets. In the presidential election year 1956, overall campaign spending in all political campaigns in the United States was estimated at $155 million, according to the Citizens' Research Foundation. Of this, only $9.8 million was used for radio and television broadcasts. Over the next decade, however, broadcasting emerged as the dominant political medium. While overall campaign spending doubled by 1968 to $300 million, broadcasting outlays increased nearly sixfold to $58.9 million.

Congressional incumbents feared that limits on media costs were needed to prevent them from draining campaign treasuries, and making candidates increasingly dependent on wealthy contributors and powerful lobbying groups. Many Democrats saw a limit on TV outlays as a way to overcome what they viewed as the Republicans' lopsided advantage in raising money.

In addition, incumbents of both parties feared that rich challengers could use TV "blitzes" to overpower them, a fear that had been fanned in 1970 by the high-cost campaigns of two relative unknowns—Rep. Richard L. Ottinger of New York and Ohio parking-lot magnate Howard M. Metzenbaum—who succeeded in winning Democratic primary races for the U.S. Senate, although they lost in the general election.

Against this backdrop of skyrocketing campaign costs, the administration of Richard Nixon tightened enforcement of the Federal Corrupt Practices Act, successfully pressing charges in 1969 against corporations (mostly in California) that had contributed money in 1968.

NOTES

1. Robert E. Mutch, *Campaigns, Congress, and Courts: The Making of Federal Campaign Finance Law* (New York: Praeger, 1988), xv.

2. George Thayer, *Who Shakes the Money Tree? American Campaign Financing Practices from 1789 to the Present* (New York: Simon and Schuster, 1973), 25.

3. Mutch, *Campaigns, Congress, and Courts*, xvi.

4. Ibid., xvii.

5. Ibid., 4.

6. Alexander Heard, *The Costs of Democracy* (Chapel Hill: University of North Carolina Press, 1960), 388.

CHAPTER 5

Reforming the System:
Laws Enacted in the 1970s

By the 1970s participants on all sides acknowledged the need for new campaign finance legislation. Within a five-year period—between 1971 and 1976—Congress passed four major laws that changed the way political campaigns for national office were financed and conducted. Stunned by the campaign abuses that came to light during the Watergate scandal, state governments and the courts also moved to alter the methods of campaign financing.

1971 REFORM LAWS

In 1971 Congress passed two separate pieces of legislation that directly affected campaign financing: the Federal Election Campaign Act (FECA) of 1971, which for the first time set a ceiling on the amount federal candidates could spend on media advertising and required full disclosure of campaign contributions and expenditures; and the Revenue Act of 1971, which included a tax checkoff section to allow taxpayers to contribute to a general public campaign fund for eligible presidential and vice presidential candidates.

FECA: Limits and Disclosure

The 1971 act was the first major piece of campaign finance legislation passed since 1925. It combined two sharply different approaches to reform. One section clamped limits on how much a federal candidate could spend on all forms of communications media. The second part provided, for the first time, for relatively complete and timely public reports by candidates on who was financing their campaigns and how much they were spending. Meaningful disclosure would reduce the likelihood of corruption and unfair advantage, it was theorized.

Media Limits. The bill went into effect April 7, 1972, sixty days after President Nixon signed it. The heart of the new law was the section placing ceilings on media costs, which was applicable separately to the primary campaign and to the general election. For a House candidate, the limit was set at $50,000 or ten cents for each voting-age person in the congressional district, whichever was greater. For a Senate candidate, the limit was $50,000 or ten cents for each voting-age person in the state.

The ceiling, which was to rise automatically with the cost of living, applied to spending for newspaper, radio, TV, magazine, billboard, and television advertising. The centerpiece of this section was the restriction that no more than 60 percent of the overall media total could go for radio and television advertising. In practice, this meant in the 1972 elections that a candiate for the House could spend no more than $52,150 for *all* media outlays in the primary campaign and no more than $52,150 in the general election campaign. (The cost-of-living factor had raised these figures from the initial $50,000.) In each case, only $31,290 of the overall media total could go for radio and television.

Because of population differences between states, the figures for Senate races ranged from an overall media limit of $52,150 in thinly populated states such as Alaska and Montana (of which only $31,290 could be for radio and TV) to as much as $1.4 million in California (of which about $850,000 could be for radio and TV).

Presidential limits also were computed on the basis of ten cents per eligible voter. For each presidential candidate, the overall media limit was $14.3 million, of which no more than $8.5 million could be used for radio and TV.

Disclosure Requirements. The 1971 FECA required that any candidate or political committee in a federal campaign file quarterly spending and receipts reports, listing contributors or recipients of $100 or more by name, place of business, and address. During election years, added reports were required to be filed fifteen and five days before an election, and any contribution of $5,000 or more had to be reported within forty-eight hours of receipt.

Closing numerous loopholes in previous law, the statute applied the reporting requirements to primaries, conventions, and runoffs as well as to the general election. Any political committee had to

report, even if it operated in only one state, provided it spent or received $1,000 or more a year. This meant, in effect, that the loophole of avoiding reports by having separate campaign fund groups in each state was eliminated for presidential candidates and that members of Congress with campaign fund groups operating only in their home states would henceforth have to report their receipts and expenditures.

The reports were to be filed with the House clerk for House candidates, secretary of the Senate for Senate candidates, and General Accounting Office (GAO) for presidential candidates. These spending and receipts reports would be made available for public inspection within forty-eight hours of being received and periodically published; reports also were required to be filed with the secretary of state of each state and made available for public inspection by the end of the day on which it was received.

On the theory that disclosure alone would eliminate corruption, all the ineffective spending and contribution limits were repealed, except provisions barring contributions directly from corporate funds and directly from union funds raised from dues money. (However, *voluntary* funds raised from union members and administered by a union unit were permitted.)

Proponents of reform, cognizant of the partisan considerations that could have threatened any revision of campaign laws, worked to avoid writing a law that would favor any political party or candidate. Republicans, aware of the relatively healthy financial condition of their party in 1971, were eager to protect their coffers; Democrats did not want to jeopardize their large contributions from organized labor.

The reform movement also included various groups outside Congress, such as the National Committee for an Effective Congress, the chief pressure group; Common Cause; labor unions; and some media organizations.

Income Tax Checkoff

The Revenue Act of 1971 containing the income tax checkoff cleared Congress on December 9, 1971, after a bitter partisan debate dominated by the approaching 1972 presidential election. President Nixon reluctantly signed the bill but forced a change in the effective date of the fund from the 1972 election to 1976 as the price of his acquiescence.

The plan gave each taxpayer the option beginning in 1973 of designating one dollar of his or her annual federal income tax payment for a general campaign fund to be divided among eligible presidential candidates. Those filing joint returns could designate two dollars.

Democrats, whose party was $9 million in debt following the 1968 presidential election, said the voluntary tax checkoff was needed to free presidential candidates from obligations to their wealthy campaign contributors. Republicans, whose party treasury was well stocked, charged that the plan was a device to rescue the Democratic party from financial difficulty.

THE WATERGATE ELECTION

Both 1971 laws were campaign finance milestones, but they left intact the existing system of private financing for the 1972 presidential campaign. While the FECA drew high marks for improving campaign disclosure and received some credit for reducing media costs, its successes were overshadowed by the massive misuse of campaign funds that characterized Watergate, one of the nation's worst political scandals.

The predominant theory at the time of passage was that merely by writing a good, tight campaign finance law emphasizing disclosure, Congress could reduce excessive contributions from any one source to any one candidate. Candidates, the theory continued, would want to avoid the appearance of being dominated by a single "big giver," which would allow the public to identify the political activities of special interest groups and take necessary corrective action at the polls.

But it did not work that way. Huge individual and corporate donations were near the center of the Watergate scandal as largely unreported private contributions financed the activities of the 1972 Nixon reelection campaign. Of the $63 million collected by the Nixon camp, nearly $20 million was in contributions from 153 donors giving $50,000 or more. More than $11 million was raised during the month before the FECA disclosure rules took effect on April 7, 1972, including $2.3 million on April 5 and $3 million on April 6.[1]

The Finance Committee for the Reelection of the President kept its pre-April 7 lists confidential until a Common Cause lawsuit sought disclosure under provisions of the old Federal Corrupt Practices Act and forced them into the open in 1973. Such reticence was partly explained by the existence of questionable contributions to the Nixon campaign: $200,000 in financier Robert Vesco's attaché case; a $100,000 secret donation from millionaire industrialist Howard Hughes, which Nixon confidant Bebe Rebozo purportedly kept locked in a safe deposit box; and $2 million pledged to Nixon by the dairy industry.

Illegal corporate gifts also motivated secrecy. In a report issued in July 1974, the Senate Select Committee on Presidential Campaign Activities (known as the Senate Watergate Committee) charged that "during the 1972 presidential campaign, it appears that at least thirteen corporations made contributions totaling over $780,000 in corporate funds.... Of these, twelve gave approximately $749,000 to the president's reelection campaign, which constituted the bulk of the illegal corporate contributions."

The primary sources of such corporate money, according to the Senate committee, were "foreign subsidiaries." Other sources included corporate reserves and expense accounts. The committee added that "although the bulk of the contributions preceded April 7, 1972, there was no disclosure of any of the contributions until July 6, 1973—or fifteen months after almost all of them were made."

Presidential lawyer Herbert Kalmbach, who headed the corporate gifts campaign, in June 1974 was sentenced to six to eighteen months in jail and fined $10,000 after pleading guilty to illegal campaign operations. Kalmbach collected more than $10 million from U.S. corporations, the bulk of it prior to April 7, 1972.

According to staff reports of the Senate Watergate Committee, Kalmbach and other fund raisers sought donations on an industry-by-industry basis, using an influential corporate executive to raise money among other executives in his industry.

The leading individual giver in the 1972 campaign was Chicago insurance executive W. Clement Stone, chairman of the Combined Insurance Co. of America. In the April 7-December 31, 1972, reporting period monitored by the GAO, Stone was listed as giving $73,054 to reelect Nixon. But even before the revelations forced by Common Cause, Stone had admitted to pre-April giving of $2 million. The second highest giver was Richard Scaife, heir to the Mellon banking and oil fortune, who contributed $1 million to Nixon's reelection before April 7.

John Gardner, then the head of Common Cause, said in April 1973:

> Watergate is not primarily a story of political espionage, nor even of White House intrigue. It is a particularly malodorous chapter in the annals of campaign financing. The money paid to the Watergate conspirators before the break-in—and the money passed to them later—was money from campaign gifts.[2]

Gardner's charge was dramatically confirmed by President Nixon's August 5, 1974, release of a June 23, 1972, tape recording of conversations between himself and his chief of staff, H. R. Haldeman. The tape revealed that Nixon was told at that time of the use of campaign funds in the June 17, 1972, Watergate break-in and agreed to help cover up that fact. Nixon's resignation August 9, 1974, followed the August 5 disclosure.

Disclosure Provisions

The campaign disclosure provisions of the 1971 FECA proved extremely useful, enabling scholars and the relevant committees of Congress to get a clear picture for the first time of patterns of contributions and spending. Emerging from the reports were data on enormous contributions by the milk industry, on corporate contributions, on formerly concealed large contributions by individuals, and on "laundered money"—information that played a key role in uncovering misconduct in the Watergate scandal.

Although thousands of reports were late or faulty, overall compliance with the disclosure law probably was fairly good. Nevertheless, a great many problems remained. The reports, especially those made in the last few days before the election, were extremely difficult for a reporter or a rival political camp to collate and decipher. Multiple contributions by a wealthy individual made to one candidate through a system of dummy organizations with cryptic names were difficult to track rapidly. Investigating an industrywide campaign of financial support to a candidate or a group of candidates proved to be an extremely tedious task.

State finance committees and other committees—with titles such as Democrats for Nixon or Writers for McGovern—were created to prevent big contributors from being inhibited by high gift taxes. An individual could give up to $3,000, tax-free, to an independent campaign committee. Records showed that the Nixon campaign benefited from 220 of these finance committees. McGovern had 785 such committees, according to his national campaign treasurer, Marian Pearlman, "created for Stewart Mott." General Motors heir Mott, who donated about $400,000 to McGovern, even declared himself a campaign committee.

The Internal Revenue Service interpreted campaign committees as being independent if one out of three officers was different from officers for other committees, if the candidates supported by the committees were different, or if the committees' purposes were different. As a result, campaign finance committees proliferated in 1972, and contributors were hardly deterred from giving large sums to one candidate.

More important, the crucial element in effectiveness of the law was enforcement. The Justice Department was given sole power to prosecute violations, despite its forty-six-year record of somnolence in enforcing previous regulations. It was traditionally understood that Justice Department bureaucrats feared to undertake vigorous enforcement lest they endanger the party in power and be fired.

The question became: Would the department make a powerful, massive effort not only to round up serious violators but to require that reports be on time and complete? Without such action from the department the practice of filing slovenly, incomplete reports, or even misleading reports, and filing them late, would clearly vitiate much of the effect of the law and render it null in practice.

Although thousands of violations—some serious but most technical (late or incomplete)—were referred to the Justice Department in 1972 and 1973 by the House and Senate and GAO, only a handful of prosecutions resulted. During the 1972 campaign the department had only one full-time attorney supervising enforcement of the act, according to reports.

Another provision in the law requiring periodic reporting of contributions and expenditures further impeded enforcement. According to many members of Congress, the frequent filing of these reports during primary and general election campaigns by all political committees of candidates created monumental bookkeeping chores for the candidates. Correspondingly, the mammoth number of reports filed with the House clerk, the Senate secretary, and the comptroller general made closer scrutiny practically impossible.

To remedy the latter problem, Common Cause, at a cost of more than $250,000 and thousands of hours from volunteer workers, organized teams of people in 1972 to collect and collate information on reports, which it then distributed to the press in time for use before election day.

Fred Wertheimer, who was then the legislative director of Common Cause, said the aim was to make the law work and to give it a good start. But it was clear that depending on private organizations alone probably would be inadequate. Unless some permanent way were found, perhaps at government expense, to speed up collation and distribution of the materials—particularly late in the campaign—the objectives of disclosure would be undermined.

Media Expenditures

The 1972 election was more expensive than any that preceded it. About $425 million was spent in all races, with the Senate Watergate Committee estimating that the presidential race cost about $100 million, more than double the $44.2 million spent in the 1968 presidential election. During the 1972 campaign, presidential and Senate outlays for radio and television campaign advertising dropped sharply compared with 1968 and 1970, but whether this decline resulted from the FECA's media advertising limits was unclear.

In the presidential race, part of the drop was due to the strength of the incumbent, who had loads of free airtime available to him when he chose to address the nation in "nonpolitical" speeches as president, instead of seeking paid time as merely a candidate.

The drop in Senate spending was less easily explained, but many senators said one factor was the realization that electronic media, while enormously effective, did not provide the quantum leap in campaigning techniques that had been expected. The notion that television could "do it all," which was virtually an article of faith in the late 1960s and in 1970, had begun to fade, and more resources were put into other forms of advertising and into traditional organizational and legwork efforts. Broadcast spending totals also were reduced by the requirement in the 1971 law that TV stations charge politicians the lowest unit rate for any time slot.

Also, many senators learned in 1972 that TV station coverage was not well designed for campaign purposes in many areas. In some large states, such as Kentucky, it was impossible to cover the whole state with stations broadcasting only within that state. To cover border areas, it was necessary to buy time on stations located in other states, only a portion of whose viewers were in Kentucky. To send a message to one corner of the state a candidate had to pay for coverage outside the state as well, a wasteful and costly practice.

The same was true in some large central metropolitan areas located between two or three states. For northern New Jersey, a candidate had to pay rates for New York too, since many of the stations in that area broadcast simultaneously to New York City, Connecticut, and northern New Jersey.

Some senators found it cheaper under these conditions to use other ways of reaching the voters. Federal Communications Commission reports showed that while a handful of senators went slightly over their campaign limits, the TV limits as a whole were observed. Because of the TV "targeting" problems, many in Congress began to argue that a flat spending limit for TV

was too inflexible. They said an overall spending limit for all campaign costs—similar to that repealed in 1971, but with real scope and enforcement teeth—would be better. Such a proposal, they argued, would still limit any massive use of TV because a candidate would not be able to exceed his total campaign spending limit. But it would allow greater flexibility as to which portion of overall costs went to TV and which to other items.

The media limits were repealed in 1974.

1974 REFORM LAW

Almost two and a half years after it passed the FECA of 1971, Congress, reacting to presidential campaign abuses and public opinion favoring reform, enacted another landmark campaign reform bill that substantially overhauled the existing system of financing election campaigns. Technically, the 1974 law was a set of amendments to the 1971 legislation, but in fact it was the most comprehensive campaign finance bill Congress had ever passed.

The new measure, which President Gerald R. Ford signed into law October 15, repealed some provisions of the 1971 law, expanded others, and broke new ground in such areas as public financing and contribution and expenditure limitations.

The Federal Election Campaign Act Amendments of 1974:

- Established a Federal Election Commission consisting of six voting members—two appointed by the president and four designated by congressional leaders—as well as two nonvoting members, the clerk of the House and secretary of the Senate. All six voting members had to be confirmed by both House and Senate.
- Instituted numerous contribution limitations,

including: for individuals, a limit of $1,000 per candidate per primary, runoff, or general election, not to exceed $25,000 to all federal candidates annually; for political committees, a limit of $5,000 per candidate per election, with no aggregate limit; for presidential and vice presidential candidates and their families, a limit of $50,000 to their own campaigns. A limit of $1,000 was established for independent expenditures on behalf of a candidate. Cash contributions of more than $100 were prohibited, as were foreign contributions in any amount.

- Set limits on spending by federal candidates and the national parties, including: a total of $10 million per candidate for all presidential primaries, $20 million per candidate in the presidential general election, and $2 million for each major political party's nominating convention and lesser amounts for minor parties' conventions; $100,000 or eight cents per eligible voter, whichever was greater, for Senate primary candidates and $150,000 or twelve cents per eligible voter, whichever was greater, for Senate general election candidates; $70,000 for House primary candidates and $70,000 for House general election candidates. National party spending was limited to $10,000 per candidate in House general elections; $20,000 or two cents per eligible voter, whichever was greater, for each candidate in Senate general elections; and two cents per voter in presidential general elections. (The party expenditures were above the candidates' individual spending limits.) Senate spending limits were applied to House candidates who represented a whole state. The act exempted certain expenditures from the limits and provided that the limits would increase with inflation. The act repealed the media spending limits adopted in 1971.
- Extended public funding for presidential cam-

paigns to include not only general election campaigns but also prenomination campaigns and national nominating conventions. Eligible candidates seeking presidential nomination would receive public funds matching their privately raised money within prescribed limits. Eligible candidates in a general election would each receive $20 million U.S. Treasury grants (to be adjusted for inflation) to finance their campaigns. Eligible political parties would receive grants of $2 million (to be adjusted for inflation) to conduct their nominating conventions. The amendments stipulated that if the level of money in the tax checkoff fund established by the 1971 Revenue Act was insufficient to finance all three stages of the electoral process, the funds would be disbursed for the general election, the conventions, and the primaries, in that order.

- Created a number of disclosure and reporting procedures, including: establishment by each candidate of one central campaign committee through which all contributions and expenditures on behalf of that candidate would be reported; reporting names and addresses, as well as occupation and place of business, of those contributing more than $100; filing of full reports of contributions and expenditures with the FEC ten days before and thirty days after each election, and within ten days of the close of each quarter. Presidential candidates were not required, however, to file more than twelve reports in any one year.

The final bill did not contain Senate-passed provisions for partial public financing of congressional campaigns. Senate conferees dropped the fight for some form of public financing for House and Senate races in return for higher spending limits for congressional campaigns and a stronger independent election commission to enforce the law.

BUCKLEY V. VALEO

As soon as the 1974 law took effect, it was challenged in court by a diverse array of plaintiffs, including Sen. James L. Buckley, C-N.Y.; former Sen. Eugene J. McCarthy, D-Minn.; the New York Civil Liberties Union; and *Human Events,* a conservative publication. They filed suit on January 2, 1975.

Their basic arguments were that the law's new limits on campaign contributions and expenditures curbed the freedom of contributors and candidates to express themselves in the political marketplace and that the public financing provisions discriminated against minor parties and lesser-known candidates in favor of the major parties and better-known candidates.

The U.S. Court of Appeals for the District of Columbia on August 14, 1975, upheld all of the law's major provisions, thus setting the stage for Supreme Court action. The Supreme Court handed down its ruling, *Buckley v. Valeo,* on January 30, 1976, in an unsigned 137-page opinion. In five separate, signed opinions, several justices concurred with and dissented from separate issues in the case.

In its decision, the Court upheld the provisions that:

- Set limits on how much individuals and political committees could contribute to candidates.
- Provided for the public financing of presidential primary and general election campaigns.
- Required the disclosure of campaign contributions of more than $100 and campaign expenditures of more than $100.

But the Court overturned other features of the law, ruling that the campaign spending limits were unconstitutional violations of the First Amendment guarantee of free expression. For presidential candidates who accepted federal matching funds, however, the ceiling on the expenditures remained intact. The Court also struck down the method for selecting members of the FEC.

Spending Limits Overturned

The Court stated: "A restriction on the amount of money a person or group can spend on political communication during a campaign necessarily reduces the quantity of expression by restricting the number of issues discussed, the depth of their exploration and the size of the audience reached. This is because virtually every means of communicating ideas in today's mass society requires the expenditure of money."

Only Justice Byron R. White dissented on this point; he would have upheld the limitations. Rejecting the argument that money is speech, White wrote that there are "many expensive campaign activities that are not themselves communicative or remotely related to speech."

Although the Court acknowledged that contribution and spending limits had First Amendment implications, it distinguished between the two by saying that the act's "expenditure ceilings impose significantly more severe restrictions on protected freedom of political expression and association than do its limitations on financial contributions."

The Court removed all the limits imposed on political spending and, by so doing, weakened the effect of the contribution ceilings. The law had placed spending limits on House, Senate, and presidential campaigns and on party nominating conventions. To plug a loophole in the contribution limits, the bill also placed a $1,000 annual limit on how much an individual could spend independently on behalf of a candidate.

The independent expenditure ceiling, the opinion said, was a clear violation of the First Amendment. The Court wrote:

While the . . . ceiling thus fails to serve any substantial government interest in stem-

ming the reality or appearance of corruption in the electoral process, it heavily burdens core First Amendment expression. . . . Advocacy of the election or defeat of candidates for federal office is not less entitled to protection under the First Amendment than the discussion of political policy generally or advocacy of the passage or defeat of legislation.

The Court also struck down the limits on how much of their own money candidates could spend on their campaigns. The law had set a $25,000 limit on House candidates, $35,000 on Senate candidates, and $50,000 on presidential candidates. "The candidate, no less than any other person, has a First Amendment right to engage in the discussion of public issues and vigorously and tirelessly to advocate his own election and the election of other candidates," the opinion said.

The ruling made it possible for a wealthy candidate to finance his own campaign and thus to avoid the limits on how much others could give him. The Court wrote that "the use of personal funds reduces the candidate's dependence on outside contributions and thereby counteracts the coercive pressures and attendant risks of abuse to which

the act's contribution limitations are directed."

Justice Thurgood Marshall rejected the Court's reasoning in striking down the limit on how much candidates may spend on their campaigns. "It would appear to follow," he said, "that the candidate with a substantial personal fortune at his disposal is off to a significant 'head start.' " Moreover, he added, keeping the limitations on contributions but not on spending "put[s] a premium on a candidate's personal wealth."

FEC Makeup Faulted

The Court held unanimously that the FEC was unconstitutional. The Court said the method for appointing commissioners violated the Constitution's separation-of-powers and appointments clauses because some members were named by congressional officials but exercised executive powers. The justices refused to accept the argument that the commission, because it oversaw congressional as well as presidential elections, could have congressionally appointed members. The Court wrote:

We see no reason to believe that the authority of Congress over federal election practices is of such a wholly different nature from the other grants of authority to Congress that it may be employed in such a manner as to offend well established constitutional restrictions stemming from the separation of powers.

According to the decision, the commission could exercise only those powers Congress was allowed to delegate to congressional committees—investigating and information-gathering. The Court ruled that only if the commission's members were appointed by the president, as required under the Constitution's appointments clause, could the commission carry out the administrative and enforcement responsibilities the law originally gave it.

The last action put Congress on the spot, because the justices stayed their ruling for thirty days, until February 29, 1976, to give the House and Senate time to "reconstitute the commission by law or adopt other valid enforcement mechanisms." As it developed, Congress was to take much longer than thirty days to act, and instead of merely reconstituting the commission, it was to pass a whole new campaign financing law.

1976 AMENDMENTS

The Court decision forced Congress to return to campaign finance legislation once again. The 1976 election campaign was already under way, but the Court said that the FEC could not continue to disburse public funds to presidential candidates so long as some commission members were congressional appointees.

President Ford had wanted only a simple reconstitution of the commission, but Congress insisted on going much further. The new law, arrived at after much maneuvering and arguing between Democrats and Republicans, closed old loopholes and opened new ones, depending on the point of view of the observer.

In its basic provision, the law signed by the president May 11, 1976, reconstituted the FEC as a six-member panel appointed by the president and confirmed by the Senate. Commission members were not allowed to engage in outside business activities. The commission was given exclusive authority to prosecute civil violations of the campaign finance law and was vested with jurisdiction over violations formerly covered only in the criminal code, thus strengthening its enforcement power.

A major controversy that delayed enactment stemmed from organized labor's insistence that corporate fund-raising activity through PACs be curtailed. Labor was angered by the FEC's SunPAC decision in November 1975 that encouraged the growth of corporate PACs.

In the wake of Watergate many corporations had been skittish about what they were permitted to do. Not until the FEC released its landmark ruling in the case involving the Sun Oil Co.'s political action committee, SunPAC, did many businesses feel comfortable in establishing PACs. The FEC decision was in response to Sun Oil's request to use general funds to create, administer, and solicit voluntary contributions to its political action committee. Besides approving the request, the decision allowed business PACs to solicit all employees and stockholders for contributions. Labor PACs had been restricted to soliciting only their members.

Eventually a compromise was reached between the Democrats, who did not hesitate to use their overwhelming numerical strength to make changes that would have severely restricted the ability of business to raise political money, and the Republicans, who lacked the strength to fend off the antibusiness amendments but had the votes to sustain a filibuster and a veto.

Labor won some but not all of its goal. The final law permitted company committees to seek contributions only from stockholders and executive and administrative personnel and their families. It continued to restrict union PACs to soliciting contributions from union members and their families. Twice a year, however, union and corporate PACs were permitted to seek campaign contributions, by mail only, from all employees. Contributions would have to remain anonymous and would be received by an independent third party that would keep records but pass the money on to the PACs.

The final bill contained another provision prompted by the Supreme Court decision. Besides finding the FEC's makeup unconstitutional, the Court had thrown out the 1974 law's limitations on independent political expenditures as a clear violation of the First Amendment. To plug the potential loophole, Congress required political committees and individuals making independent political expenditures of more than $100 to swear that the expenditures were not made in collusion with the candidate.

The 1976 legislation also set some new contribution limits: An individual could give no more than $5,000 a year to a PAC and $20,000 to the national committee of a political party (the 1974 law set a $1,000 per election limit on individual contributions to a candidate and an aggregate contribution limit for individuals of $25,000 a year; no specific limits, except the aggregate limit, applied to contributions to political committees). A PAC could give no more than $15,000 a year to the national committee of a political party (the 1974 law set only a limit of $5,000 per election per candidate). The Democratic and Republican senatorial campaign committees could give up to $17,500 a year to a candidate (the 1974 law had set a $5,000 per election limit).

HILL PUBLIC FUNDING DEFEATED

Following the 1976 election, the spotlight in campaign finance quickly focused on extending public financing to House and Senate races. Prospects for passage seemed far better than they had been in 1974, the last time the proposal had been considered. At that time, leading officials, from the White House on down, had been either opposed or seemingly indifferent to its passage.

But in 1977 Jimmy Carter, a strong advocate of public funding, was in the White House. Key congressional leaders favored the proposal. And the Democrats had an overwhelming advantage in the House, far larger than during the 93rd Congress (1973-75), when the House rejected congressional public financing after it had been approved by the Senate.

Despite the high hopes of public financing supporters, legislation to extend the concept to congressional races was blocked in 1977 by a filibuster in the Senate and opposition in the House Administration Committee. Renewed attempts to push the legislation in 1978 and 1979 also went nowhere.

After public funding's defeat in 1979, supporters of campaign finance reform tried unsuccessfully to reduce PAC contributions to House candidates. They won House passage in 1979, but the bill died in the Senate the following year. Although the bill applied only to House races, opponents in the Senate feared that its passage could renew interest in public financing or could lead to PAC spending ceilings in Senate races.

1979 FECA AMENDMENTS

In a rare demonstration of harmony on a campaign finance measure, Congress in late 1979 passed legislation to eliminate much of the red tape created by the FECA and to encourage political party activity. Agreement was not difficult because the drafters concentrated on solving FECA's noncontroversial problems.

The amendments reduced FECA's paperwork

requirements in several ways. First, the act decreased the maximum number of reports a federal candidate would have to file with the FEC during a two-year election cycle from twenty-four to nine. Second, candidates who raised or spent less than $5,000 in their campaigns would not have to file reports at all. In 1978 about seventy House candidates, including five winners, fell below the $5,000 threshold. Previously, all candidates were required to report their finances regardless of the amount. Also, candidates would have to report in less detail. The legislation raised the threshold for itemizing both contributions and expenditures to $200 from $100.

In 1976 political party leaders had complained that the FECA almost completely precluded state and local party organizations from helping with the presidential campaign. Because they had only limited federal funds to spend, both the Democratic and Republican presidential campaigns focused on media advertising. At the same time, they cut back expenditures on items such as buttons and bumper stickers that traditionally were used in promoting grass-roots activity.

The 1979 bill permitted state and local party groups to purchase, without limit, campaign materials for volunteer activities to promote any federal candidate. Those items included buttons, bumper stickers, handbills, brochures, posters, and yard signs. Also, those party organizations were allowed to conduct, without financial limit, certain kinds of voter registration and get-out-the-vote drives on behalf of presidential tickets.

The incidental mention of a presidential candidate on the campaign literature of local candidates was no longer counted as a campaign contribution. Previously, such references had been counted, which created paperwork problems in reporting those costs to the FEC. Local party groups would be required to report their finances only if annual spending for volunteer activities exceeded $5,000 or if costs for nonvolunteer projects were more than $1,000. Before, such groups had to file campaign reports if total spending exceeded $1,000 a year.

Volunteer political activity by individuals was encouraged by raising to $1,000, from $500, the amount of money a person could spend in providing his home, food, or personal travel on behalf of a candidate without reporting it to the FEC as a contribution. If the volunteer activity was on behalf of a political party, the person could spend up to $2,000 before the amount was treated as a contribution.

NOTES

1. Herbert E. Alexander, *Financing the 1972 Election* (Lexington, Mass.: D. C. Heath, 1976), 7.
2. *Facts on File,* April 29-May 5, 1973, 357.

CHAPTER 6

Campaign Reform Proposals:
Congressional Stalemate

Congress repeatedly visited the issue of campaign finance reform in the 1980s but failed to pass any major legislation. Reform fell victim to differences both between the parties and within the parties over what was wrong with the system and how it should be remedied.

PAC LIMITS STALLED IN 1986

After legislation limiting PAC spending had died in the Senate in 1980, several years passed before the issue was debated again. But the rise in the number of PACs and their influence in political campaigns continued to put lawmakers on the defensive against a public perception that special interest groups had undue influence on politicians.

The Senate went on record twice in 1986 in favor of strict new controls on campaign fund raising. The Senate first adopted an amendment offered by the Democrats that would have set caps on what a candidate could take from PACs overall and singly and also would have closed loopholes on PAC giving that generally favored Republicans. The Senate then adopted a Republican counterproposal to prohibit PAC contributions to national

party organizations, which Democrats relied on more heavily than the GOP. But the legislation ended up mired in partisan maneuvering over who should get the credit—or blame—for reforming campaign finance guidelines, and which party would suffer the most under the proposed restrictions. A final vote was never taken.

COMPREHENSIVE BILL
DIES IN 1988

The most comprehensive campaign finance bill to come before Congress since 1974 was shelved after a record-setting eight cloture votes in 1987-88 failed to cut off a Republican filibuster in the Senate.

The cornerstone of the Democrats' bill was a proposal for overall campaign spending limits, specified on a state-by-state basis, which backers saw as the key to curbing skyrocketing election costs. But such limits were bitterly opposed by Republicans, who thought a spending cap would institutionalize the Democrats' majority in Congress. Another key element that many Republicans abhorred was a provision for public financing for

Senate candidates who agreed to abide by the spending limits. Most Republicans said it represented a government intrusion into what generally had been a private realm. Republicans also criticized the bill's aggregate limit on what Senate candidates could accept from PACs on the ground that the provision would favor the well-organized, well-funded PACs that could donate early in an election cycle, freezing out other PACs that wanted to donate later.

The protracted debate over the bill was marked by extraordinary partisanship and elaborate par-

R. Michael Jenkins

Sen. David L. Boren, D-Okla., left, has led efforts to overhaul the campaign finance system. Sen. Mitch McConnell, R-Ky., led a Republican filibuster against Democratic campaign finance legislation in 1988. The Democrats tried, and failed, to shut off debate a record eight times in 1987-88.

liamentary maneuvering. Majority Leader Robert Byrd attempted to break the GOP filibuster by keeping the Senate in session around the clock. During one of two all-night sessions Republicans responded in kind, by repeatedly moving for quorum calls and then boycotting the floor. That forced Democrats to keep enough members present to maintain the quorum needed for the Senate to remain in session. Byrd then decided to resort to a little-known power of the Senate, last used in 1942, to have absent members arrested and brought to the floor. This led to the spectacle of Oregon Republican Bob Packwood being arrested and physically carried onto the Senate floor in the wee hours of February 24, 1988.

A truce was eventually reached, the final unsuccessful cloture vote taken, and the bill was pulled from the floor. A later attempt to adopt a constitutional amendment to overcome the *Buckley v. Valeo* decision forbidding mandatory campaign spending limits suffered a similar fate.

IMPASSE AGAIN IN 1990

The movement in the next Congress to rewrite campaign finance laws ended where it began, mired in disagreement. The House and Senate passed separate bills—both generally backed by Democrats and strongly opposed by Republicans—aimed at reducing campaign spending and limiting the influence of PACs. But President Bush threatened to veto any bill with campaign spending limits, and with ideological and political differences too wide to bridge late in the session, conferees on the two bills never met.

Bush in 1989 had proposed what he called a "sweeping system of reform" that sought to eliminate most PACs, enhance the role of political parties, and grind down the electoral advantages enjoyed by incumbents (including one of the major weapons in an incumbent's arsenal, the frank, by

Campaign Cash Loophole Closed

One of Congress's most elite groups became a disappearing species in 1989, when Congress closed a loophole that had allowed senior House members to pocket leftover campaign funds after they left Congress.

The loophole had been a target for reformers who accused members of using their campaign kitties as a unique form of individual retirement account. It had also created resentment among senators and younger House members who could not take advantage of it.

The loophole had been opened by a provision of the 1979 campaign law amendments that had barred personal use of excess campaign funds, except by "grandfathered" members—those who were in the House on January 8, 1980, even if they left and returned later. Under House rules, they could make personal use of the money only after leaving Congress. Once they disclosed its conversion, their reporting obligations ended, although it was considered taxable income. Senate rules flatly prohibited personal use by members past or present.

But in 1989 Congress adopted a provision in an ethics-and-pay law that forced the grandfathered House members to choose: leave Congress before the beginning of the 103rd Congress in 1993, or lose their right to take the money. The funds that could be converted were frozen at no more than what they had on hand when the 1989 ethics law was enacted.

At the beginning of the 101st Congress in 1989, 191 House members were eligible to take advantage of this grandfather clause. That left 244 who could not.

A Congressional Quarterly review of federal campaign records showed it was a lucrative loophole, with "grandfathered" ex-members converting to personal use at least $862,000 between 1980 and the beginning of 1989. More than $710,000 of this was in cash. Another $115,000 was either borrowed or used to retire personal loans unconnected to their former campaigns. At least $37,000 went for cars, furniture, travel, and other services.

Source: Congressional Quarterly Almanac 1989, 55.

banning "unsolicited mass mailings" from congressional offices). Democrats had assailed the Bush plan as baldly partisan. Even within the GOP, there had been no consensus on major items such as curbing the frank and eliminating certain PACs.

The bill the Senate passed in 1990 would have dismantled PACs and created a system of voluntary spending limits for Senate elections with incentives such as discounted broadcast rates and reduced postage for campaign mailings, as well as public funding for a candidate whose opponent broke the spending limit.

The 1990 House bill also would have created voluntary spending limits, but would have imposed a flat cap of $550,000 for a House candidate's

primary and general election combined, instead of establishing limits on a state-by-state basis as the Senate bill would have. The House bill included incentives for complying with the limits, but public funding was not among them. Rather than eliminate PACs, the House measure would have divided them into two categories, dependent upon the size of donations the PACs received from their members, and set different limits for candidate contributions from the two groups. Aggregate limits would have been placed on the money candidates could accept from PACs.

Besides the difference between the two chambers' treatment of PACs, the bills were wide apart on the issue of soft money—the unregulated millions of dollars unions, corporations, individuals, and PACs donated to political parties for election-related activities. The Senate would have taken a big step toward imposing federal rules on state election activities; the House limited itself primarily to abuses that cropped up in the 1988 presidential campaigns. Both bills also would have set new restrictions on the practice of bundling political contributions and on independent expenditures.

With campaign finance overhaul presumed dead for the year, lawmakers late in the session peeled off the one part of the effort that every politician could agree on: getting broadcasters to lower advertising rates for candidates. A Federal Communications Commission study had found that candidates were paying higher prices than commercial advertisers at a majority of thirty radio and television stations in five metropolitan areas. But neither chamber acted on the proposal because the effort encountered opposition not only from broadcasters but also from Common Cause, which said the legislation would provide a major benefit to incumbents without dealing with the fundamental problems in the campaign finance system.

UPHILL BATTLE

Efforts at reform were renewed in the next Congress, but the gaps between the parties and the chambers were still present at the outset, leaving many wondering when, or if, the partisan breakthrough necessary to make a new law would come.

The Senate moved first, passing a bill in May 1991. The measure imposed state-by-state limits on Senate campaigns by offering candidates incentives, including public financing and discounted broadcast advertising rates, to participate. It also banned PAC contributions to all federal candidates.

In many ways, the Senate debate was a replay of the 1990 debate. Democrats argued that spending limits were the only way to hold down the

rising cost of campaigns and to end "the money chase." And they held out spending limits and public financing as a way to level the playing field for candidates challenging incumbents. Republicans sought to undercut spending limits, calling them a device that would hamstring challengers who needed to outspend an incumbent to win. Moreover, they argued that the bill's benefits were a hammer held over the heads of candidates to coerce them into giving up the right to spend freely in campaigns. But with Democrats solid on the need for spending limits, the Republicans zeroed in on the more vulnerable target of public financing. They belittled it as "food stamps for politicians" and questioned the willingness of taxpayers—only one in five of whom were then designating money from their taxes for public financing of presidential elections—to expand the program.

House debate on their campaign finance bill also echoed the partisan 1990 debate. The House measure, which passed in November 1991, set voluntary spending limits in primary and general elections. Candidates who agreed to comply with the limits would get benefits, including cut-rate postage and limited public financing. The bill also scaled back the amount of money that PACs would be able to give candidates. Like their Senate counterparts, House Republicans attacked the bill's public financing provisions, saying the taxpayers would end up picking up the tab.

The drastic differences in the House and Senate bills promised a difficult conference in 1992. Although the Republicans have an ace in the hole—George Bush, who has promised to veto any legislation that calls for public financing or spending limits—the Democrats will charge the president with hypocrisy for accepting public funding for his own campaign but rejecting the idea of partial public funding in congressional elections. The current campaign finance system is probably here to stay until the same party controls both the White House and Congress.

Appendix

APPENDIX

The Federal Election Campaign Act:

Tested and Changed

Congress in early 1972 cleared the first comprehensive political campaign financing law since the unenforced Corrupt Practices Act of 1925. The Supreme Court January 30, 1976, held unconstitutional major portions of the legislation, called the Federal Election Campaign Act (FECA) of 1971, which had been amended in 1974.

A suit challenging the constitutionality of provisions of the law had been brought by James L. Buckley, C-N.Y., then a senator, and by Eugene J. McCarthy, D-Minn., who retired from the Senate in 1971 and ran for president as an independent candidate in 1976. The suit challenged provisions of the law that set campaign contribution and spending limits and that established disclosure requirements. It also challenged the appointment by Congress of some of the members of the Federal Election Commission (FEC), which was charged with administering the act. Moreover, the suit challenged the constitutionality of provisions that authorized public financing of presidential campaigns and of party nominating conventions.

The Supreme Court held in the case, *Buckley v. Valeo* (Francis R. Valeo was then secretary of the Senate), that the FEC was improperly ap-

pointed since four of its six members had been appointed by Congress. Appointment of some of the panel's members by Congress, rather than by the president, the Court ruled, was unconstitutional. In its opinion, the Court pointed to the "concern of the Framers of the Constitution with maintenance of the separation of powers . . . ." Article II, Section 2, clause 2 of the Constitution provides that officers of the United States be appointed by the president (with the advice and consent of the Senate in the case of superior officers). The Court did not accept the argument of the appellants that the FEC, because it oversaw congressional as well as presidential elections, could include members appointed by Congress. However, the Court held that the FEC's past actions had de facto validity.

Court Findings

The Supreme Court upheld the act's limits on the size of individual and political committee campaign contributions. The challengers had contended that limits on how much individuals and groups could give to political campaigns violated their First Amendment right to freedom of speech. The Court, with two justices dissenting, held that such limits entail "only a marginal restriction upon the contributor's ability to engage in free communication."

The Court also sustained the act's provisions for public disclosure of campaign contributions. The challengers had not attacked disclosure directly but had claimed that the law hurt minor party and independent candidates by requiring that too much be disclosed.

Provisions of the act limiting expenditures for presidential, Senate, and House campaigns were found unconstitutional except in the case of presidential candidates who accepted federal matching funds. The Court said the although both contribution and spending limits have First Amendment implications, the act's "expenditure ceilings impose significantly more severe restrictions on protected freedom of political expression and association than do its limitations on financial contributions." The Court also ruled against the act's limits on how much of their own money candidates for federal office could spend on their campaigns. Another spending limit found to be unconstitutional was one on independent expenditures—the amount groups or individuals who were not candidates could spend in advocating a candidate's election so long as the expenditures were not controlled by or coordinated with the candidate.

The Court upheld public financing of presidential elections and national party nominating conventions and asserted that the use of public money to subsidize candidates did not favor established parties over new parties or incumbents over challengers. The formula for distributing the public funds, the Court said, "is a congressional effort, not to abridge, restrict or censor speech, but rather to use public money to facilitate and enlarge public discussion and participation in the electoral process." The act's provisions for matching federal grants to finance presidential primary campaigns was also upheld.

Action by Congress

The Court's ruling put immediate pressure on Congress to pass new legislation to provide a flow of federal funds to the 1976 presidential candidates. Congress responded to the Supreme Court's decision with a major revision of the campaign finance law. The new measure, the Federal Election Campaign Finance Act Amendments of 1976, was signed into law by President Gerald R. Ford May 11 of that year. The law reconstituted the FEC with all six of its members nominated by the president and confirmed by the Senate and with its enforcement powers strengthened. Some changes were made in the definitions and limits on campaign contributions although the aggregate contribution limit for individuals was not changed. The new law placed restrictions on the fundraising activities of corporate and union political action committees.

Disclosure provisions were amended to require candidates and political committees to keep records of contributions of $50 or more rather than $10 or more as provided in the 1974 law. It also required political committees and individuals making an independent political expenditure of more than $100 to file a report with the FEC. Presidential candidates who accepted public financing were limited to spending no more than $50,000 of their own or their family's money. The new law did not change the public financing provisions for presidential campaigns or spending limits for presidential campaigns.

Shortly before the 1980 presidential election year began, Congress enacted the 1979 amendments to the FECA, without opposition in either house. President Jimmy Carter signed the bill into law on January 8, 1980. The amendments were designed to be "noncontroversial" to ensure passage, and many of the provisions resulted in technical fine-tuning of the FECA after flaws and problems with it became obvious during the 1976 and 1978 elections. The new law's significance was that it represented some backtracking from the earlier stringent reform positions and some lightening of the burdens upon practitioners. Yet some changes were extensive. Essentially the bill simplified record-keeping and public reporting requirements, increased the permissible role of state and local political parties, and refined the procedural requirements of the enforcement process.

In the pages that follow are excerpts from the *Buckley v. Valeo* decision, as well as summaries of the major provisions of the 1971 Federal Election Campaign Act, the related 1971 Revenue Act, and the FECA amendments of 1974, 1976, and 1979.

BUCKLEY V. VALEO

Following are excerpts from the Supreme Court's opinion, decided January 30, 1976, on the constitutionality of the Federal Election Campaign Act of 1971, as amended in 1974, and from the opinions, dissenting in part and concurring in part, of Chief Justice Warren E. Burger and Associate Justices Byron R. White, Thurgood Marshall, Harry A. Blackmun, and William H. Rehnquist:

Nos. 75-436 and 75-437

James L. Buckley et al.,
    Appellants,
       75-436 *v.*
Francis R. Valeo,
Secretary of the United
    States Senate,
      et al.

On Appeal from the
United States Court of
Appeals for the
District of Columbia
Circuit.

James L. Buckley et al.,
    Appellants,
       75-437 *v.*
Francis R. Valeo,
Secretary of the United
    States Senate,
      et al.

On Appeal from the
United States District
Court for the District
of Columbia.

PER CURIAM. [MR. JUSTICE STEVENS took no part in the consideration or decision of these cases.]

These appeals present constitutional challenges to the key provisions of the Federal Election Campaign Act of 1971, as amended in 1974.

The Court of Appeals, in sustaining the Act in large part against various constitutional challenges, viewed it as "by far the most comprehensive reform legislation [ever] passed by Congress concerning the election of the President, Vice-President, and members of Congress." . . . The Act, summarized in broad terms, contains the following provisions: (a) individual political contributions are limited to $1,000 to any single candidate per election, with an overall annual limitation of $25,000 by any contributor; independent expenditures by individuals and groups "relative to a clearly identified candidate" are limited to $1,000 a year; campaign spending by candidates for various federal offices and spending for national conventions by political parties are subject to prescribed limits; (b) contributions and expenditures above certain threshold levels must be reported and publicly disclosed; (c) a system for public funding of Presidential campaign activities is established by Subtitle H of the Internal Revenue Code; and (d) a Federal Election Commission is established to administer and enforce the Act. . . .

. . . On plenary review, a majority of the Court of Appeals rejected, for the most part, appellants' constitutional attacks. The court found "a clear and compelling interest," 519 F. 2d, at 841, in preserving the integrity of the electoral process. On that basis, the court upheld, with one exception, the substantive provisions of the Act with respect to contributions, expenditures and disclosure. It also sustained the constitutionality of the newly established Federal Election Commission. The court concluded that, notwithstanding the manner of selection of its members and the breadth of its powers, which included nonlegislative functions, the Commission is a constitutionally authorized agency created to perform primarily legislative functions. The provisions for public funding of the three stages of the Presidential selection process were upheld as a valid exercise of congressional power under the General Welfare Clause of the Constitution, Art. I, § 8.

In this Court, appellants argue that the Court of Appeals failed to give this legislation the critical scrutiny demanded under accepted First Amendment and equal protection principles. In appellants' view, limiting the use of money for political purposes constitutes a restriction on communication violative of the First Amendment, since virtually all meaningful political communications in the modern setting involve the expenditure of money. Further, they argue that the reporting and disclosure provisions of the Act unconstitutionally impinge on their right to freedom of association. Appellants also view the federal subsidy provisions of Subtitle H as violative of the General Welfare Clause, and as inconsistent with the First and Fifth Amendments. Finally, appellants renew their attack on the Commission's composition and powers.

At the outset we must determine whether the case before us presents a "case or controversy" within the meaning of Art. III of the Constitution. Congress may not, of course, require this Court to render opinions in matters which are not "cases and controversies." ...We must therefore decide whether appellants have the "personal stake in the outcome of the controversy" necessary to meet the requirements of Art. III.... It is clear that Congress, in enacting [the Federal Election Campaign Act], intended to provide judicial review to the extent permitted by Art. III. In our view, the complaint in this case demonstrates that at least some of the appellants have a sufficient "personal stake" in a determination of the constitutional validity of each of the challenged provisions to

present "a real and substantial controversy admitting of specific relief through a decree of a conclusive character, as distinguished from an opinion advising what the law would be upon a hypothetical state of facts." *Aetna Life Insurance Co. v. Haworth,* [1937]. ...

I. CONTRIBUTION AND EXPENDITURE LIMITATIONS

The intricate statutory scheme adopted by Congress to regulate federal election campaigns includes restrictions on political contributions and expenditures that apply broadly to all phases of and all participants in the election process. The major contribution and expenditure limitations in the Act prohibit individuals from contributing more than $25,000 in a single year or more than $1,000 to any single candidate for an election campaign and from spending more than $1,000 a year "relative to a clearly identified candidate." Other provisions restrict a candidate's use of personal and family resources in his campaign and limit the overall amount that can be spent by a candidate in campaigning for federal office.

The constitutional power of Congress to regulate federal elections is well established and is not questioned by any of the parties in this case. Thus, the critical constitutional questions presented here go not to the basic power of Congress to legislate in this area, but to whether the specific legislation that Congress has enacted interferes with First Amendment freedoms or invidiously discriminates against nonincumbent candidates and minor parties in contravention of the Fifth Amendment.

A. General Principles

The Act's contribution and expenditure limitations operate in an area of the most fundamental First Amendment activities. Discussion of public issues and debate on the qualifications of candidates are integral to the operation of the system of government established by our Constitution. The First

Amendment affords the broadest protection to such political expression in order "to assure the unfettered interchange of ideas for the bringing about of political and social changes desired by the people." *Roth v. United States* . . . (1957). . . . "[T]here is practically universal agreement that a major purpose of th[e] Amendment was to protect the free discussion of governmental affairs, . . . of course includ[ing] discussions of candidates. . . ." *Mills v. Alabama* . . . (1966). . . .

The First Amendment protects political association as well as political expression. The constitutional right of association explicated in *NAACP v. Alabama* . . . (1958), stemmed from the Court's recognition that "[e]ffective advocacy of both public and private points of view, particularly controversial ones, is undeniably enhanced by group association." Subsequent decisions have made clear that the First and Fourteenth Amendments guarantee "freedom to associate with others for the common advancement of political beliefs and ideas," a freedom that encompasses "[t]he right to associate with the political party of one's choice." *Kusper v. Pontikes* . . . (1973). . . .

It is with these principles in mind that we consider the primary contentions of the parties with respect to the Act's limitations upon the giving and spending of money in political campaigns. Those conflicting contentions could not more sharply define the basic issues before us. Appellees contend that what the Act regulates is conduct, and that its effect on speech and association is incidental at most. Appellants respond that contributions and expenditures are at the very core of political speech, and that the Act's limitations thus constitute restraints on First Amendment liberty that are both gross and direct.

In upholding the constitutional validity of the Act's contribution and expenditure provisions on the ground that those provisions should be viewed as regulating conduct not speech, the Court of Appeals relied upon *United States v. O'Brien* . . . (1968). . . .

. . . Even if the categorization of the expenditure of money as conduct were accepted, the limitations challenged here would not meet the *O'Brien* test because the governmental interests advanced in support of the Act involve "suppressing communication." The interests served by the Act include restricting the voices of people and interest groups who have money to spend and reducing the overall scope of federal election campaigns. Although the Act does not focus on the ideas expressed by persons or groups subjected to its regulations, it is aimed in part at equalizing the relative ability of all voters to affect electoral outcomes by placing a ceiling on expenditures for political expression by citizens and groups. . . .

. . . A restriction on the amount of money a person or group can spend on political communication during a campaign necessarily reduces the quantity of expression by restricting the number of issues discussed, the depth of their exploration, and the size of the audience reached. This is because virtually every means of communicating ideas in today's mass society requires the expenditure of money. The distribution of the humblest handbill or leaflet entails printing, paper, and circulation costs. Speeches and rallies generally necessitate hiring a hall and publicizing the event. The electorate's increasing dependence on television, radio, and other mass media for news and information has made these expensive modes of communication indispensable instruments of effective political speech.

The expenditure limitations contained in the Act represent substantial rather than merely theoretical restraints on the quantity and diversity of political speech. The $1,000 ceiling on spending "relative to a clearly identified candidate," . . . would appear to exclude all citizens and groups except candidates, political parties and the institutional press from any significant use of the most effective modes of communication. Although the Act's limitations on expenditures by campaign organizations and political parties provide substantially greater room for discussion and debate, they would have required restrictions in the scope of a number of past congressional and Presidential campaigns and would operate to constrain campaigning by candidates who raise sums in excess of the spending ceiling.

By contrast with a limitation upon expenditures for political expression, a limitation upon the amount that any one person or group may contribute to a candidate or political committee entails only a marginal restriction upon the contributor's ability to engage in free communication. A contribution serves as a general expression of support for the candidate and his views, but does not communicate the underlying basis for the support. The quantity of communication by the contributor does not increase perceptibly with the size of his contribution, since the expression rests solely on the undifferentiated, symbolic art of contributing. At most, the size of the contribution provides a very rough index of the intensity of the contributor's support for the candidate. A limitation on the amount of money a person may give to a candidate or campaign organization thus involves little direct restraint on his political communication, for it permits the symbolic expression of support evidenced by a contribution but does not in any way infringe the contributor's freedom to discuss candidates and issues. While contributions may result in political expression if spent by a candidate or an association to present views to the voters, the transformation of contributions into political debate involves speech by someone other than the contributor.

Given the important role of contributions in financing political campaigns, contribution restrictions could have a severe impact on political dialogue if the limitations prevented candidates and political committees from amassing the resources necessary for effective advocacy. There is no indication, however, that the contribution limitations imposed by the Act would have any dramatic adverse effect on the funding of campaigns and political associations. The overall effect of the Act's contribution ceilings is merely to require candidates and political committees to raise funds from a greater number of persons and to compel people who would otherwise contribute amounts greater than the statutory limits to expend such funds on

direct political expression, rather than to reduce the total amount of money potentially available to promote political expression.

The Act's contribution and expenditure limitations also impinge on protected associational freedoms. Making a contribution, like joining a political party, serves to affiliate a person with a candidate. In addition, it enables like-minded persons to pool their resources in furtherance of common political goals. The Act's contribution ceilings thus limit one important means of associating with a candidate or committee, but leave the contributor free to become a member of any political association and to assist personally in the association's efforts on behalf of candidates. And the Act's contribution limitations permit associations and candidates to aggregate large sums of money to promote effective advocacy. By contrast, the Act's $1,000 limitation on independent expenditures "relative to a clearly identified candidate" precludes most associations from effectively amplifying the voice of their adherents, the original basis for the recognition of First Amendment protection of the freedom of association. . . .

In sum, although the Act's contribution and expenditure limitations both implicate fundamental First Amendment interests, its expenditure ceilings impose significantly more severe restrictions on protected freedoms of political expression and association than do its limitations on financial contributions.

B. Contribution Limitations

1. The $1,000 Limitation on Contributions by Individuals and Groups to Candidates and Authorized Campaign Committees

Section 608 (b) provides, with certain limited exceptions, that "no person shall make contributions to any candidate with respect to any election for Federal office which, in the aggregate, exceeds $1,000." The statute defines person broadly to include "an individual, partnership, committee, association, corporation, or any other organization or group of persons." . . . The limitation reaches a gift, subscription, loan, advance, deposit of anything of value, or promise to give a contribution, made for the purpose of influencing a primary election, a Presidential preference primary, or a general election for any federal office. . . . The $1,000 ceiling applies regardless of whether the contribution is given to the candidate, to a committee authorized in writing by the candidate to accept contributions on his behalf, or indirectly via earmarked gifts passed through an intermediary to the candidate. . . . The restriction applies to aggregate amounts contributed to the candidate for each election — with primaries, runoff elections, and general elections counted separately and all Presidential primaries held in any calendar year treated together as a single election campaign. . . .

Appellants contend that the $1,000 contribution ceiling unjustifiably burdens First Amendment freedoms, employs overbroad dollar limits, and discriminates against candidates opposing incumbent officeholders and against minor-party candidates in violation of the Fifth Amendment. We address each of these claims of invalidity in turn.

(a) . . . [T]he primary First Amendment problem raised by the Act's contribution limitations is their restriction of one aspect of the contributor's freedom of political association. The Court's decisions involving associational freedoms establish that the right of association is a "basic constitutional freedom" that is "closely allied to freedom of speech and a right which, like free speech, lies at the foundation of a free society. . . . In view of the fundamental nature of the right to associate, governmental "action which may have the effect of curtailing the freedom to associate is subject to the closest scrutiny." *NAACP v. Alabama, supra*. . . . Yet, it is clear that "[n]either the right to associate nor the right to participate in political activities is absolute. . . ." *Civil Service Comm'n v. Letter Carriers* . . . (1973). Even a " 'significant interference' with protected rights of political association" may be sustained if the State demonstrates a sufficiently important interest and employs means closely drawn to avoid unnecessary abridgment of associational freedoms. . . .

Appellees argue that the Act's restrictions on large campaign contributions are justified by three governmental interests. According to the parties and *amici,* the primary interest served by the limitations and, indeed, by the Act as a whole, is the prevention of corruption and the appearance of corruption spawned by the real or imagined coercive influence of large financial contributions on candidates' positions and on their actions if elected to office. Two "ancillary" interests underlying the Act are also allegedly furthered by the $1,000 limits on contributions. First, the limits serve to mute the voices of affluent persons and groups in the election process and thereby to equalize the relative ability of all citizens to affect the outcome of elections. Second, it is argued, the ceilings may to some extent act as a brake on the skyrocketing cost of political campaigns and thereby serve to open the political system more widely to candidates without access to sources of large amounts of money.

It is unnecessary to look beyond the Act's primary purpose . . . in order to find a constitutionally sufficient justification for the $1,000 contribution limitation. Under a system of private financing of elections, a candidate lacking immense personal or family wealth must depend on financial contributions from others to provide the resources necessary to conduct a successful campaign. The increasing importance of the communications media and sophisticated mass mailing and polling operations to effective campaigning make the raising of large sums of money an ever more essential ingredient of an effective candidacy. To the extent that large contributions are given to secure political *quid pro quos* from current and potential office holders, the integrity of our system of representative democracy is undermined. Although the scope of such pernicious practices can never be reliably ascertained, the deeply disturbing examples surfacing after the 1972 election demonstrate that the problem is not an illusory one.

Of almost equal concern as the danger of actual *quid pro quo* arrangements is the impact of the appearance of corruption stemming from public awareness of the opportunities for abuse inherent in a regime of large individual financial contributions. . . .

Appellants contend that the contribution limitations must be invalidated because bribery laws and narrowly-drawn disclosure requirements constitute a less restrictive means of dealing with "proven and suspected *quid pro quo* arrangements." But laws making criminal the giving and taking of bribes deal with only the most blatant and specific attempts of those with money to influence governmental action. And while disclosure requirements serve the many salutary purposes discussed elsewhere in this opinion, Congress was surely entitled to conclude that disclosure was only a partial measure, and that contribution ceilings were a necessary legislative concomitant to deal with the reality or appearance of corruption inherent in a system permitting unlimited financial contributions, even when the identities of the contributors and the amounts of their contributions are fully disclosed.

The Act's $1,000 contribution limitation focuses precisely on the problem of large campaign contributions — the narrow aspect of political association where the actuality and potential for corruption have been identified — while leaving persons free to engage in independent political expression, to associate actively through volunteering their services, and to assist to a limited but nonetheless substantial extent in supporting candidates and committees with financial resources. Significantly, the Act's contribution limitations in themselves do not undermine to any material degree the potential for robust and effective discussion of candidates and campaign issues by individual citizens, associations, the institutional press, candidates, and political parties.

We find that, under the rigorous standard of review established by our prior decisions, the weighty interests served by restricting the size of financial contributions to political candidates are sufficient to justify the limited effect upon First Amendment freedoms caused by the $1,000 contribution ceiling.

(b) Appellants' first overbreadth challenge to the contribution ceilings rests on the proposition that most large contributors do not seek improper influence over a candidate's position or an officeholder's action. Although the truth of that proposition may be assumed, it does not undercut the validity of the $1,000 contribution limitation. Not only is it difficult to isolate suspect contributions but, more importantly, Congress was justified in concluding that the interest in safeguarding against the appearance of impropriety requires that the opportunity for abuse inherent in the process of raising large monetary contributions be eliminated.

A second, related overbreadth claim is that the $1,000 restriction is unrealistically low because much more than that amount would still not be enough to enable an unscrupulous contributor to exercise improper influence over a candidate or officeholder, especially in campaigns for statewide or national office. While the contribution limitation provisions might well have been structured to take account of the graduated expenditure limitations for House, Senate and Presidential campaigns, Congress' failure to engage in such fine tuning does not invalidate the legislation. . . .

(c) Apart from these First Amendment concerns, appellants argue that the contribution limitations work such an invidious discrimination between incumbents and challengers that the statutory provisions must be declared unconstitutional on their face. In considering this contention, it is important at the outset to note that the Act applies the same limitations on contributions to all candidates regardless of their present occupations, ideological views, or party affiliations. Absent record evidence of invidious discrimination against challengers as a class, a court should generally be hesitant to invalidate legislation which on its face imposes evenhanded restrictions. . . .

There is no such evidence to support the claim that the contribution limitations in themselves discriminate against major-party challengers to incumbents. Challengers can and often do defeat incumbents in federal elections. . . .

. . . The charge of discrimination against minor-party and independent candidates is more troubling, but the record provides no basis for concluding that the Act invidiously disadvantages such candidates. As noted above, the Act on its face treats all candidates equally with regard to contribution limitations. And the restriction would appear to benefit minor-party and independent candidates relative to their major-party opponents because major-party candidates receive far more money in large contributions. . . .

In view of these considerations, we conclude that the impact of the Act's $1,000 contribution limitation on major-party challengers and on minor-party candidates does not render the provision unconstitutional on its face.

2. The $5,000 Limitation on Contributions by Political Committees

Section 608 (b)(2) of Title 18 permits certain committees, designated as "political committees," to contribute up to $5,000 to any candidate with respect to any election for federal office. In order to qualify for the higher contribution ceiling, a group must have been registered with the Commission as a political committee . . . for not less than 6 months, have received contributions from more than 50 persons and, except for state political party organizations, have contributed to five or more candidates for federal office. Appellants argue that these qualifications unconstitutionally discriminate against ad hoc organizations in favor of established interest groups and impermissibly burden free association. The argument is without merit. Rather than undermining freedom of association, the basic provision enhances the opportunity of bona fide groups to participate in the election process, and the registration, contribution, and candidate conditions serve the permissible purpose of preventing individuals from evading the applicable contribution limitations by labeling themselves committees.

3. Limitations on Volunteers' Incidental Expenses

The Act excludes from the definition of contribution "the value of services provided without compensation by individuals who volunteer a portion or all of their time on behalf of a candidate or political committee." . . . Certain expenses incurred by persons in providing volunteer services to a candidate are exempt from the $1,000 ceiling only to the extent that they do not exceed $500. . . .

If, as we have held, the basic contribution limitations are constitutionally valid, then surely these provisions are a constitutionally acceptable accommodation of Congress' valid interest in encouraging citizen participation in political campaigns while continuing to guard against the corrupting potential of large financial contributions to candidates. The expenditure of resoures at the candidate's direction for a fundraising event at a volunteer's residence or the provision of in-kind assistance in the form of food or beverages to be resold to raise funds or consumed by the participants in such an event provides material financial assistance to a candidate. . . . Treating these expenses as contributions when made to the candidate's campaign or at the direction of the candidate or his staff forecloses an avenue of abuse without limiting actions voluntarily undertaken by citizens independently of a candidate's campaign.

4. The $25,000 Limitation on Total Contributions During any Calendar Year

In addition to the $1,000 limitation on the nonexempt contributions that an individual may make to a particular candidate for any single election, the Act contains an overall $25,000 limitation on total contributions by an individual during any calendar year. . . . The overall $25,000 ceiling does impose an ultimate restriction upon the number of candidates and committees with which an individual may associate himself by means of financial support. But this quite modest restraint upon protected political activity serves to prevent evasion of the $1,000 contribution limitation by a person who might otherwise contribute massive amounts of money to a particular candidate through the use of unearmarked contributions to political committees likely to contribute to that candidate, or huge contributions to the candidate's political party. The limited, additional restriction on associational freedom imposed by the overall ceiling is thus no more than a corollary of the basic individual contribution limitation that we have found to be constitutionally valid.

C. Expenditure Limitations

The Act's expenditure ceilings impose direct and substantial restraints on the quantity of political speech. The most drastic of the limitations restricts individuals and groups, including political parties that fail to place a candidate on the ballot, to an expenditure of $1,000 "relative to a clearly identified candidate during a calendar year." § 608 (e)(1) Other expenditure ceilings limit spending by candidates ... their campaigns ... and political parties in connection with election campaigns.... It is clear that a primary effect of these expenditure limitations is to restrict the quantity of campaign speech by individuals, groups, and candidates. The restrictions, while neutral as to the ideas expressed, limit political expression "at the core of our electoral process and of First Amendment freedoms...." *Williams v. Rhodes* ... (1968).

1. The $1,000 Limitation on Expenditures "Relative to a Clearly Identified Candidate"

... The plain effect [of this limitation] is to prohibit all individuals, who are neither candidates nor owners of institutional press facilities, and all groups, except political parties and campaign organizations, from voicing their views "relative to a clearly identified candidate" through means that entail aggregate expenditures of more than $1,000 during a calendar year. The provision, for example, would make it a federal criminal offense for a person or association to place a single one-quarter page advertisement "relative to a clearly identified candidate" in a major metropolitan newspaper.

Before examining the interests advanced in support of [this] expenditure ceiling, consideration must be given to appellants' contention that the provision is unconstitutionally vague....

... [I]n order to preserve the provision against invalidation on vagueness grounds, [this limitation] must be construed to apply only to expenditures for

communications that in express terms advocate the election or defeat of a clearly identified candidate for federal office.

... We turn ... to the basic First Amendment question — whether [this limitation], even as thus narrowly and explicitly construed, impermissibly burdens the constitutional right of free expression....

... [T]he constitutionality of [this limitation] turns on whether the governmental interests advanced in its support satisfy the exacting scrutiny applicable to limitations on core First Amendment rights of political expression.

We find that the governmental interest in preventing corruption and the appearance of corruption is inadequate to justify [the] ceiling on independent expenditures. First, assuming *arguendo* that large independent expenditures pose the same dangers of actual or apparent *quid pro quo* arrangements as do large contributions, § 608 (e)(1) does not provide an answer that sufficiently relates to the elimination of those dangers. Unlike the contribution limitations' total ban on the giving of large amounts of money to candidates, § 608 (e)(1) prevents only some large expenditures. So long as persons and groups eschew expenditures that in express terms advocate the election or defeat of a clearly identified candidate, they are free to spend as much as they want to promote the candidate and his views. The exacting interpretation of the statutory language necessary to avoid unconstitutional vagueness thus undermines the limitation's effectiveness as a loophole-closing provision by facilitating circumvention by those seeking to exert improper influence upon a candidate or officeholder. It would naively underestimate the ingenuity and resourcefulness of persons and groups desiring to buy influence to believe that they would have much difficulty devising expenditures that skirted the restriction on express advocacy of election or defeat but nevertheless benefited the candidate's campaign. Yet no substantial societal interest would be served by a loophole-closing provision designed to check corruption that permitted unscrupulous persons and organizations to expend unlimited sums of money in order to obtain improper influence over candidates for elective office. . . .

Second, quite apart from the shortcomings of § 608 (e)(1) in preventing any abuses generated by large independent expenditures, the independent advocacy restricted by the provision does not presently appear to pose dangers of real or apparent corruption comparable to those identified with large campaign contributions. The parties defending § 608 (e)(1) contend that it is necessary to prevent would-be contributors from avoiding the contribution limitations by the simple expedient of paying directly for media advertisements or for other portions of the candidate's campaign activities. They argue that expenditures controlled by or coordinated with the candidate and his campaign might well have virtually the same value to the candidate as a contribution and would pose similar dangers of abuse. Yet such controlled or coordinated expenditures are treated as contributions rather than expenditures under the Act. . . . Unlike contributions, such independent expenditures may well provide little assistance to the candidate's campaign and indeed may prove counterproductive. The absence of prearrangement and coordination of an expenditure with the candidate or his agent not only undermines the value of the expenditure to the candidate, but also alleviates the danger that expenditures will be given as a *quid pro quo* for improper commitments from the candidate. Rather than preventing circumvention of the contribution limitations, § 608 (e)(1) severely restricts all independent advocacy despite its substantially diminished potential for abuse.

While the independent expenditure ceiling thus fails to serve any substantial governmental interest in stemming the reality or appearance of corruption in the electoral process, it heavily burdens core First Amendment expression. . . . Advocacy of the election or defeat of candidates for federal office is no less entitled to protection under the First Amendment than the discussion of political policy generally or advocacy of the passage or defeat of legislation.

It is argued, however, that the ancillary governmental interest in equalizing the relative ability of individuals and groups to influence the outcome of elections serves to justify the limitation on express advocacy of the election or defeat of candidates imposed by [the] expenditure ceiling. But the concept that government may restrict the speech of some elements of our society in order to enhance the relative voice of others is wholly foreign to the First Amendment. . . . The First Amendment's protection against governmental abridgement of free expression cannot properly be made to depend on a person's financial ability to engage in public discussion. . . .

. . . For the reasons stated, we conclude that [the] independent expenditure limitation is unconstitutional under the First Amendment.

2. Limitation on Expenditures by Candidates from Personal or Family Resources

The Act also sets limits on expenditures by a candidate "from his personal funds, or the personal funds of his immediate family, in connection with his campaigns during any calendar year." . . . These ceilings vary from $50,000 for Presidential or Vice Presidential candidates to $35,000 for Senate candidates, and $25,000 for most candidates for the House of Representatives.

The ceiling on personal expenditure by candidates on their own behalf, like the limitations on independent expenditures . . . imposes a substantial restraint on the ability of persons to engage in protected First Amendment expression. The candidate, no less than any other person, has a First Amendment right to engage in the discussion of public issues and vigorously and tirelessly to advocate his own election and the election of other candidates. Indeed, it is of particular importance that candidates have the unfettered opportunity to make their views known so that the electorate may intelligently evaluate the candidates' personal qualities and their positions on vital public issues before choosing among them on election day. . . . [The] ceiling on personal expenditures by a candidate in furtherance of his own candidacy thus clearly and directly interferes with constitutionally protected freedoms.

The primary governmental interest served by the Act — the prevention of actual and apparent corruption of the political process — does not support the limitation on the candidate's expenditure of his own personal funds. . . . Indeed, the use of personal funds reduces the candidate's dependence on outside contributions and thereby counteracts the coercive pressures and attendant risks of abuse to which the Act's contribution limitations are directed.

The ancillary interest in equalizing the relative financial resources of candidates competing for elective office . . . is clearly not sufficient to justify the provision's infringement of fundamental First Amendment rights. First, the limitation may fail to promote financial equality among candidates. A candidate who spends less of his personal resources on his campaign may nonetheless outspend his rival as a result of more successful fundraising efforts. . . . Second, and more fundamentally, the First Amendment simply cannot tolerate . . . [a] restriction upon the freedom of a candidate to speak without legislative limit on behalf of his own candidacy. We therefore hold that . . . [the] restrictions on a candidate's personal expenditures is [sic] unconstitutional.

3. Limitations on Campaign Expenditures

Section 608 (c) of the Act places limitations on overall campaign expenditures by candidates seeking nomination for election and election to federal office. Presidential candidates may spend $10,000,000 in seeking nomination for office and an additional $20,000,000 in the general election campaign. . . . The ceiling on Senate campaigns is pegged to the size of the voting age population of the State with minimum dollar amounts applicable to campaigns in States with small populations. In Senate primary elections, the limit is the greater of eight cents multiplied by the voting age population or $100,000, and in the general election the limit is increased to 12 cents multiplied by the voting age population or $150,000. . . . The Act imposes blanket $70,000 limitations on both primary campaigns and general election campaigns for the House of Representatives with the exception that the Senate ceiling applies to campaigns in States entitled to only one Representative. . . . These ceilings are to be adjusted upwards at the beginning of each calendar year by the average percentage rise in the consumer price index for the 12 preceding months. . . .

No governmental interest that has been suggested is sufficient to justify the restriction on the quantity of political expression imposed by § 608 (c)'s campaign expenditure limitations. The major evil associated with rapidly increasing campaign expenditures is the danger of candidate dependence on large contributions. The interest in alleviating the corrupting influence of large contributions is served by the Act's contribution limitations and disclosure provisions. . . . The Court of Appeal's assertion that the expenditure restrictions are necessary to reduce the incentive to circumvent direct contribution limits is not persuasive. . . .

The interest in equalizing the financial resources of candidates competing for federal office is no more convincing a justification for restricting the scope of federal election campaigns. Given the limitation on the size of outside contributions, the financial resources available to a candidate's campaign, like the number of volunteers recruited, will normally vary with the size and intensity of the candidate's support. . . .

The campaign expenditure ceilings appear to be designed primarily to serve the governmental interests in reducing the allegedly skyrocketing costs of political campaigns. . . . [T]he mere growth in the cost of federal election campaigns in and of itself provides no basis for governmental restrictions on the quantity of campaign spending and the resulting limitations on the scope of federal campaigns. The First Amendment denies government the power to determine that spending to promote one's political views is wasteful, excessive, or unwise. . . .

For these reasons we hold that § 608 (c) is constitutionally invalid.

In sum, the provisions of the Act that impose a $1,000 limitation on contributions to a single candidate, § 608 (b)(1), a $5,000 limitation on contributions by a political committee to a single candidate, § 608 (b)(2), and a $25,000 limitation on total contributions by an individual during any calendar year, § 608 (b)(3), are constitutionally valid. These limitations along with the disclosure provisions, constitute the Act's primary weapons against the reality or appearance of improper influence stemming from the dependence of candidates on large campaign contributions. The contribution ceilings thus serve the basic governmental interest in safeguarding the integrity of the electoral process without directly impinging upon the rights of individual citizens and candidates to engage in political debate and discussion. By contrast, the First Amendment requires the invalidation of the Act's independent expenditure ceiling, § 608 (e)(1), its limitation on a candidate's expenditures from his own personal funds, § 608 (c). These provisions place substantial and direct restrictions on the ability of candidates, citizens, and associations to engage in protected political expression, restrictions that the First Amendment cannot tolerate.

II. REPORTING AND DISCLOSURE REQUIREMENTS

Unlike the limitations on contributions and expenditures, . . . the disclosure requirements of the Act . . . are not challenged by appellants as *per se* unconstitutional restrictions on the exercise of First Amendment freedoms of speech and association. Indeed, appellants argue that "narrowly drawn disclosure requirements are the proper solution to virtually all of the evils Congress sought to remedy." The particular requirements embodied in the Act are attacked as overbroad — both in their application to minor-party and independent candidates and in their extension to contributions as small as $10 or $100. Appellants also challenge the provision for disclosure by those who make independent contributions and expenditures. . . .

. . . The Act presently under review replaced all prior disclosure laws. Its primary disclosure provi-

sions impose reporting obligations on "political committees" and candidates. "Political committee" is defined . . . as a group of persons that receives "contributions" or makes "expenditures" of over $1,000 in a calendar year. "Contributions" and "expenditures" are defined in lengthy parallel provisions similar to those . . . discussed above. Both definitions focus on the use of money or other objects of value "for the purpose of influencing" the nomination or election of any person to federal office. . . .

Each political committee is required to register with the Commission . . . and to keep detailed records of both contributions and expenditures. . . . These records are required to include the name and address of everyone making a contribution in excess of $10, along with the date and amount of the contribution. If a person's contributions aggregate more than $100, his occupation and principal place of business are also to be included. . . . These files are subject to periodic audits and field investigations by the Commission. . . .

Each committee and each candidate also is required to file quarterly reports. . . . The reports are to contain detailed financial information, including the full name, mailing address, occupation, and principal place of business of each person who has contributed over $100 in a calendar year, as well as the amount and date of the contributions. . . . They are to be made available by the Commission "for public inspection and copying." . . . Every candidate for Federal office is required to designate a "principal campaign committee," which is to receive reports of contributions and expenditures made on the candidate's behalf from other political committees and to compile and file these reports, together with its own statements, with the Commission. . . .

Every individual or group, other than a political committee or candidate, who makes "contributions" or "expenditures" of over $100 in a calendar year "other than by contribution to a political committee or a candidate" is required to file a statement with the Commission. . . . Any violation of these record-keeping and reporting provisions is punishable by a fine of not more than $1,000 or a prison term of not more than a year, or both. . . .

A. General Principles

Unlike the overall limitations on contributions and expenditures, the disclosure requirements impose no ceiling on campaign-related activities. But we have repeatedly found that compelled disclosure, in itself, can seriously infringe on privacy of association and belief guaranteed by the First Amendment. . . .

We long have recognized that significant encroachments on First Amendment rights of the sort that compelled disclosure imposes cannot be justified by a mere showing of some legitimate governmental interest. . . . [W]e have required that the subordinating interests of the State must survive exacting scrutiny. We also have insisted that there be a "relevant correlation" or "substantial relation" between the governmental interest and the information required to be disclosed. . . .

. . . [C]ompelled disclosure has the potential for substantially infringing the exercise of First Amendment rights. But we have acknowledged that there are governmental interests sufficiently important to outweigh the possibility of infringement, particularly when the "free functioning of our national institutions" is involved. . . .

The governmental interests sought to be vindicated by the disclosure requirements are of this magnitude. They fall into three categories. First, disclosure provides the electorate with information "as to where political campaign money comes from and how it is spent by the candidate" in order to aid the voters in evaluating those who seek Federal office. . . .

Second, disclosure requirements deter actual corruption and avoid the appearance of corruption by exposing large contributions and expenditures to the light of publicity. This exposure may discourage those who would use money for improper purposes either before or after the election. . . .

Third, and not least significant, record-keeping, reporting and disclosure requirements are an es-

sential means of gathering the data necessary to detect violations of the contribution limitations described above.

The disclosure requirements, as a general matter, directly serve substantial governmental interests. In determining whether these interests are sufficient to justify the requirements we must look to the extent of the burden that they place on individual rights.

It is undoubtedly true that public disclosure of contributions to candidates and political parties will deter some individuals who otherwise might contribute. In some instances, disclosure may even expose contributors to harassment or retaliation. These are not insignificant burdens on individual rights, and they must be weighed carefully against the interests which Congress has sought to promote by this legislation. . . . [W]e . . . agree with appellants' concession that disclosure requirements — certainly in most applications — appear to be the least restrictive means of curbing the evils of campaign ignorance and corruption that Congress found to exist. Appellants argue, however, that the balance tips against disclosure when it is required of contributors to certain parties and candidates. We turn now to this contention.

B. Application to Minor Parties and Independents

Appellants contend that the Act's requirements are overbroad insofar as they apply to contributions to minor parties and independent candidates because the governmental interest in this information is minimal and the danger of significant infringement on First Amendment rights is greatly increased.

1. Requisite Factual Showing

. . . It is true that the governmental interest in disclosure is diminished when the contribution in question is made to a minor party with little chance of winning an election. As minor parties usually represent definite and publicized viewpoints, there may be less need to inform the voters of the interests that specific candidates represent. . . .

. . . But a minor party sometimes can play a significant role in an election. Even when a minor-party candidate has little or no chance of winning, he may be encouraged by major-party interests in order to divert votes from other major-party contenders.

We are not unmindful that the damage done by disclosure to the associational interests of the minor parties and their members and to supporters of independents could be significant. . . . In some instances fears of reprisal may deter contributions to the point where the movement cannot survive. The public interest also suffers if that result comes to pass, for there is a consequent reduction in the free circulation of ideas both within and without the political arena.

There could well be a case . . . where the threat to the exercise of First Amendment rights is so serious and the state interest furthered by disclosure so insubstantial that the Act's requirements cannot be constitutionally applied. But no appellant in this case has tendered record evidence of [this] sort. . . .

2. Blanket Exemption

Appellants agree that "the record here does not reflect the kind of focused and insistent harassment of contributors and members that existed in the NAACP cases." They argue, however, that a blanket exemption for minor parties is necessary lest irreparable injury be done before the required evidence can be gathered. . . .

. . . We recognize that unduly strict requirements of proof could impose a heavy burden, but it does not follow that a blanket exemption for minor parties is necessary. Minor parties must be allowed sufficient flexibility in the proof of injury to assure a fair consideration of their claim. The evidence offered need show only a reasonable probability that the compelled disclosure of a party's contributors' names will subject them to threats, harassment or reprisals from either government officials or private parties. . . .

C. Section 434 (e)

Section 434 (e) requires "[e]very person (other than a political committee or candidate) who makes contributions or expenditures" aggregating over $100 in a calendar year "other than by contribution to a political committee or candidate" to file a statement with the Commission. Unlike the other disclosure provisions, this section does not seek the contribution list of any association. Instead, it requires direct disclosure of what an individual or group contributes or spends.

In considering this provision we must apply the same strict standard of scrutiny, for the right of associational privacy developed in *Alabama* derives from the rights of the organization's members to advocate their personal points of view in the most effective way. . . .

Appellants attack § 434 (e) as a direct intrusion on privacy of belief, in violation of *Talley v. California* . . . (1960), and as imposing "very real, practical burdens . . . certain to deter individuals from making expenditures for their independent political speech" analogous to those held to be impermissible in *Thomas v. Collins* . . . (1945).

1. The Role of § 434 (e)

. . . Section 434 (e) is part of Congress' effort to achieve "total disclosure" by reaching "every kind of political activity" in order to insure that the voters are fully informed and to achieve through publicity the maximum deterrence to corruption and undue influence possible. The provision is responsive to the legitimate fear that efforts would be made, as they had been in the past, to avoid the disclosure requirements by routing financial support of candidates through avenues not explicitly covered by the general provisions of the Act.

2. Vagueness Problems

In its effort to be all-inclusive, however, the provision raises serious problems of vagueness, particularly treacherous where, as here, the violation of its terms carries criminal penalties and fear of incurring these sanctions may deter those who seek to exercise protected First Amendment rights.

Section 434 (e) applies to "[e]very person . . .

who makes contributions or expenditures." "Contributions" and "expenditures" are defined in parallel provisions in terms of the use of money or other valuable assets "for the purpose of ... influencing" the nomination or election of candidates for Federal office. It is the ambiguity of this phrase that poses constitutional problems. ...

... To insure that the reach of § 434 (e) is not impermissibly broad, we construe "expenditure" for purposes of that section in the same way we construed the terms of § 608 (e) — to reach only funds used for communications that expressly advocate the election or defeat of a clearly identified candidate. This reading is directed precisely to that spending that is unambiguously related to the campaign of a particular federal candidate.

In summary, § 434 (e) as construed imposes independent reporting requirements on individuals and groups that are not candidates or political committees only in the following circumstances: (1) when they make contributions earmarked for political purposes or authorized or requested by a candidate or his agent, to some person other than a candidate or political committee, and (2) when they make an expenditure for a communication that expressly advocates the election or defeat of a clearly identified candidate.

Unlike § 608 (e)(1), § 434 (e) as construed bears a sufficient relationship to a substantial governmental interest. ... It goes beyond the general disclosure requirements to shed the light of publicity on spending that is unambiguously campaign-related but would not otherwise be reported because it takes the form of independent expenditures or of contributions to an individual or group not itself required to report the names of its contributors. ...

... [T]he disclosure requirement is narrowly limited to those situations where the information sought has a substantial connection with the governmental interests sought to be advanced. ... The burden imposed by § 434 (e) is no prior restraint, but a reasonable and minimally restrictive method of furthering First Amendment values by opening the basic processes of our federal election system to public view.

D. Thresholds

Appellants' third contention, based on alleged overbreadth, is that the monetary thresholds in the record-keeping and reporting provisions lack a substantial nexus with the claimed governmental interests, for the amounts involved are too low even to attract the attention of the candidate, much less have a corrupting influence.

The provisions contain two thresholds. Records are to be kept by political committees of the names and addresses of those who make contributions in excess of $10 ... and these records are subject to Commission audit. ... If a persons' contributions to a committee or candidate aggregate more than $100, his name and address, as well as his occupation and principal place of business, are to be included in reports filed by committees and candidates with the Commission ... and made available for public inspection. ...

... The $10 and $100 thresholds are indeed low. ... These strict requirements may well discourage participation by some citizens in the political process, a result that Congress hardly could have intended. Indeed, there is little in the legislative history to indicate that Congress focused carefully on the appropriate level at which to require recording and disclosure. Rather, it seems merely to have adopted the thresholds existing in similar disclosure laws since 1910. But we cannot require Congress to establish that it has chosen the highest reasonable threshold. ...

We are mindful that disclosure serves informational functions, as well as the prevention of corruption and the enforcement of the contribution limitations. Congress is not required to set a threshold that is tailored only to the latter goals. ...

... [T]here is no warrant for assuming that public disclosure of contributions between $10 and $100 is authorized by the Act. Accordingly, we do not reach the question whether information concerning gifts of this size can be made available to the public without trespassing impermissibly on First Amendment rights. ...

In summary, we find no constitutional infirmities in the record-keeping, reporting, and disclosure provisions of the act.

III. PUBLIC FINANCING OF PRESIDENTIAL ELECTION CAMPAIGNS

A series of statutes for the public financing of Presidential election campaigns produced the scheme now found in 26 U.S.C. § 6096 and Subtitle H, §§ 9001-9042, of the Internal Revenue Code of 1954. Both the District Court ... and the Court of Appeals ... sustained Subtitle H against a constitutional attack. Appellants renew their challenge here, contending that the legislation violates the First and Fifth Amendments. We find no merit in their claims and affirm.

A. Summary of Subtitle H

Section 9006 establishes a Presidential Election Campaign Fund, financed from general revenues in the aggregate amount designated by individual taxpayers, under § 6096, who on their income tax returns may authorize payment to the Fund of one dollar of their tax liability in the case of an individual return or two dollars in the case of a joint return. The Fund consists of three separate accounts to finance (1) party nominating conventions, ... (2) general election campaigns, ... and (3) primary campaigns....

Chapter 95 of Title 26, which concerns financing of party nominating conventions and general election campaigns, distinguishes among "major," "minor" and "new" parties. A major party is defined as a party whose candidate for President in the most recent election received 25% or more of the popular vote.... A minor party is defined as a party whose candidate received at least 5% but less than 25% of the vote at the most recent election.... All other parties are new parties, ... including both newly created parties and those receiving less than 5% of the vote in the last election.

Major parties are entitled to $2,000,000 to defray their national committee Presidential nomi-

nating convention expenses, must limit total expenditures to that amount ... and they may not use any of this money to benefit a particular candidate or delegate.... A minor party receives a portion of the major-party entitlement determined by the ratio of the votes received by the party's candidate in the last election to the average of the votes received by the major-parties' candidates.... The amounts given to the parties and the expenditure limit are adjusted for inflation, using 1974 as the base year.... No financing is provided for new parties, nor is there any express provision for financing independent candidates or parties not holding a convention.

For expenses in the general election campaign, § 9004 (a)(1) entitles each major-party candidate to $20,000,000. This amount is also adjusted for inflation.... To be eligible for funds the candidate must pledge not to incur expenses in excess of the entitlement under § 9004 (a)(1) and not to accept private contributions except to the extent that the fund is insufficient to provide the full entitlement.... Minor-party candidates are also entitled to funding, again based on the ratio of the vote received by the party's candidate in the preceding election to the average of the major-party candidates.... Minor-party candidates must certify that they will not incur campaign expenses in excess of the major-party entitlement and that they will accept private contributions only to the extent needed to make up the difference between that amount and the public funding grant.... New-party candidates receive no money prior to the general election, but any candidate receiving 5% or more of the popular vote in the election is entitled to post-election payments according to the formula applicable to minor-party candidates.... Similarly, minor-party candidates are entitled to post-election funds if they receive a greater percentage of the average major-party vote than their party's candidate did in the preceding election; the amount of such payments is the difference between the entitlement based on the preceding election and that based on the actual vote in the current election.... A further eligibility requirement for minor- and new-party candidates is that the candidate's name must appear on the ballot, or electors pledged to the candidate must be on the ballot, in at least 10 States. . . .

Chapter 96 establishes a third account in the Fund, the Presidential Primary Matching Payment Account. . . . This funding is intended to aid campaigns by candidates seeking Presidential nomination "by a political party," . . . in "primary elections,". . . . The threshold eligibility requirement is that the candidate raise at least $5,000 in each of 20 States, counting only the first $250 from each person contributing to the candidate. . . . In addition, the candidate must agree to abide by the spending limits. . . . Funding is provided according to a matching formula: each qualified candidate is entitled to a sum equal to the total private contributions received, disregarding contributions from any person to the extent that total contributions to the candidate by that person exceed $250. . . . Payments to any candidate under Chapter 96 may not exceed 50% of the overall expenditure ceiling accepted by the candidate. . . .

B. Constitutionality of Subtitle H

Appellants argue that Subtitle H is invalid (1) as "contrary to the 'general welfare,' " Art. I, § 8, (2) because any scheme of public financing of election campaigns is inconsistent with the First Amendment, and (3) because Subtitle H invidiously discriminates against certain interests in violation of the Due Process Clause of the Fifth Amendment. We find no merit in these contentions.

Appellants' "general welfare" contention erroneously treats the General Welfare Clause as a limitation upon congressional power. It is rather a grant of power, the scope of which is quite expansive, particularly in view of the enlargement of power by the Necessary and Proper Clause. . . . Congress has power to regulate Presidential elections and primaries, . . . and public financing of Presidential elections as a means to reform the electoral process was clearly a choice within the granted power. It is for Congress to decide which

expenditures will promote the general welfare. "[T]he power of Congress to authorize expenditure of public moneys for public purposes is not limited by the direct grants of legislative power found in the Constitution." *United States v. Butler* . . . (1936). . . . Any limitations upon the exercise of that granted power must be found elsewhere in the Constitution. In this case, Congress was legislating for the "general welfare" — to reduce the deleterious influence of large contributions on our political process, to facilitate communication by candidates with the electorate, and to free candidates from the rigors of fundraising. . . . Whether the chosen means appear "bad," "unwise," or "unworkable" to us is irrelevant; Congress has concluded that the means are "necessary and proper" to promote the general welfare, and we thus decline to find this legislation without the grant of power in Art. I, § 8.

Appellants' challenge to the dollar check-off provision (§ 6096) fails for the same reason. They maintain that Congress is required to permit taxpayers to designate particular candidates or parties as recipients of their money. But the appropriation to the Fund in § 9006 is like any other appropriation from the general revenue except that its amount is determined by reference to the aggregate of the one- and two-dollar authorization on taxpayers' income tax returns. . . .

Appellants next argue that "by analogy" to the religion clauses of the First Amendment public financing of election campaigns, however meritorious, violates the First Amendment. . . . But the analogy is patently inapplicable to our issue here. Although "Congress shall make no law . . . abridging the freedom of speech, or of the press," Subtitle H is a congressional effort, not to abridge, restrict, or censor speech, but rather to use public money to facilitate and enlarge public discussion and participation in the electoral process, goals vital to a self-governing people. . . . Appellants argue, however, that as constructed public financing invidiously discriminates in violation of the Fifth Amendment. We turn therefore to that argument. . . .

. . . .[T]he denial of public financing to some Presidential candidates is not restrictive of voters' rights and less restrictive of candidates'. Subtitle H does not prevent any candidate from getting on the ballot or any voter from casting a vote for the candidate of his choice; the inability, if any, of minority-party candidates to wage effective campaigns will derive not from lack of public funding but from their inability to raise private contributions. Any disadvantages suffered by operation of the eligibility formulae under Subtitle H is thus limited to the claimed denial of the enhancement of opportunity to communicate with the electorate that the formula affords eligible candidates. But eligible candidates suffer a countervailing denial. As we more fully develop later, acceptance of public financing entails voluntary acceptance of an expenditure ceiling. Noneligible candidates are not subject to that limitation. Accordingly, we conclude that public financing is generally less restrictive of access to the electoral process than the ballot-access regulations dealt with in prior cases. In any event, Congress enacted Subtitle H in furtherance of sufficiently important governmental interests and has not unfairly or unnecessarily burdened the political opportunity of any party or candidate.

. . . [P]ublic financing as a means of eliminating the improper influence of large private contributions furthers a significant governmental interest. . . . In addition, . . . Congress properly regarded public financing as an appropriate means of relieving major-party Presidential candidates from the rigors of soliciting private contributions. . . . Congress' interest in not funding hopeless candidacies with large sums of public money . . . necessarily justifies the withholding of public assistance from candidates without significant public support. . . .

1. General Election Campaign Financing

Appellants insist that Chapter 95 falls short of the constitutional requirement in that the provisions provide larger, and equal, sums to candidates of major parties, use prior vote levels as the sole criterion for pre-election funding, limit new-party candidates to post-election funds, and deny any funds to candidates of parties receiving less than 5% of the vote. These provisions, it is argued, are fatal to the validity of the scheme, because they work invidious discrimination against minor and new parties in violation of the Fifth Amendment. We disagree. . . .

. . . Since the Presidential elections of 1856 and 1860, when the Whigs were replaced as a major party by the Republicans, no third party has posed a credible threat to the two major parties in Presidential elections. Third parties have been completely incapable of matching the major parties' ability to raise money and win elections. Congress was of course aware of this fact of American life, and thus was justified in providing both major parties full funding and all other parties only a percentage of the major-party entitlement. Identical treatment of all parties, on the other hand, "would not only make it easy to raid the United States Treasury, it would also artificially foster the proliferation of splinter parties.". . .

Furthermore, appellants have made no showing that the election funding plan disadvantages nonmajor parties by operating to reduce their strength below that attained without any public financing. . . . Thus, we conclude that the general election funding system does not work an invidious discrimination against candidates of nonmajor parties.

Appellants challenge reliance on the vote in past elections as the basis for determining eligibility. That challenge is foreclosed, however, by our holding in *Jenness v. Fortson* . . . [1971] that popular vote totals in the last election are a proper measure of public support. . . .

. . . Any risk of harm to minority interests is speculative due to our present lack of knowledge of the practical effects of public financing and cannot overcome the force of the governmental interests against use of public money to foster frivolous candidacies, create a system of splintered parties, and encourage unrestrained factionalism. . . .

. . . Plainly campaigns can be successfully carried out by means other than public financing; they have been up to this date, and this avenue is still open to all candidates. And, after all, the important achievements of minority political groups in furthering the development of American democracy were accomplished without the help of public funds. Thus, the limited participation or nonparticipation of nonmajor parties or candidates in public funding does not unconstitutionally disadvantage them. . . .

. . . Finally, appellants challenge the validity of the 5% threshold requirement for general election funding. They argue that, since most state regulations governing ballot access have threshold requirements well below 5%, and because in their view the 5% requirement here is actually stricter than that upheld in *Jenness v. Fortson* . . . the requirement is unreasonable. . . . [T]he choice of the percentage requirement that best accommodates the competing interests involved was for Congress to make. . . . Without any doubt a range of formulations would sufficiently protect the public fisc and not foster factionalism, and also recognize the public interest in the fluidity of our political affairs. We cannot say that Congress' choice falls without the permissible range.

2. Nominating Convention Financing

The foregoing analysis and reasoning sustaining general election funding apply in large part to convention funding under Chapter 95 and suffices to support our rejection of appellants' challenge to that provision. Funding of party conventions has increasingly been derived from large private contributions . . . and the governmental interest in eliminating this reliance is as vital as in the case of private contributions to individual candidates. The expenditure limitations on major parties participating in public financing enhance the ability of nonmajor parties to increase their spending relative to the major parties; further, in soliciting private contributions to finance conventions, parties are not subject to the $1,000 contribution limit pertaining to candidates. We therefore conclude that appellants' constitutional challenge to the provisions for funding nominating conventions must also be rejected.

3. Primary Election Campaign Financing

Appellants' final challenge is to the constitution-ality of Chapter 96, which provides funding of primary campaigns. They contend that these provisions are constitutionally invalid (1) because they do not provide funds for candidates not running in party primaries and (2) because the eligibility formula actually increases the influence of money on the electoral process. In not providing assistance to candidates who do not enter party primaries, Congress has merely chosen to limit at this time the reach of the reforms encompassed in Chapter 96. This Congress could do without constituting the reform a constitutionally invidious discrimination. . . .

. . . We also reject as without merit appellants' argument that the matching formula favors wealthy voters and candidates. The thrust of the legislation is to reduce financial barriers and to enhance the importance of smaller contributions. . . . In addition, one eligibility requirement for matching funds is acceptance of an expenditure ceiling, and candidates with little fundraising ability will be able to increase their spending relative to candidates capable of raising large amounts in private funds.

For the reasons stated, we reject appellants' claims that Subtitle H is facially unconstitutional.

C. Severability

The only remaining issue is whether our holdings invalidating §§ 608 (a), 608 (c), and 608 (e)(1) require the conclusion that Subtitle H is unconstitutional. There is of course a relationship between the spending limits in 18 U.S.C. § 608 (c) and the public financing provisions; the expenditure limits accepted by a candidate to be eligible for public funding are identical to the limits in § 608 (c). But we have no difficulty in concluding that Subtitle H is severable. . . . Our discussion . . . leaves no doubt that the value of public financing is not dependent on the existence of a generally applicable expenditure limit. We therefore hold Subtitle H severable from those portions of the legislation today held constitutionally infirm.

IV. THE FEDERAL ELECTION COMMISSION

The 1974 Amendments to the Act created an eight-member Federal Election Commission, and vest in it primary and substantial responsibility for administering and enforcing the Act. The question that we address in this portion of the opinion is whether, in view of the manner in which a majority of its members are appointed, the Commission may under the Constitution exercise the powers conferred upon it. . . .

Chapter 14 of Title 2 makes the Commission the principal repository of the numerous reports and statements which are required by that Chapter to be filed by those engaging in the regulated political activities. Its duties . . . with respect to these reports and statements include filing and indexing, making them available for public inspection, preservation, and auditing and field investigations. It is directed to "serve as a national clearinghouse for information in respect to the administration of elections.". . .

Beyond these recordkeeping, disclosure, and investigative functions, however, the Commission is given extensive rulemaking and adjudicative powers. . . .

The Commission's enforcement power is both direct and wide-ranging. . . .

. . . The body in which this authority is reposed consists of eight members. The Secretary of the Senate and the Clerk of the House of Representatives are *ex officio* members of the Commission without the right to vote. Two members are appointed by the President *pro tempore* of the Senate "upon the recommendations of the majority leader of the Senate and the minority leader of the Senate." Two more are to be appointed by the Speaker of the House of Representatives, likewise upon the recommendations of its respective majority and minority leaders. The remaining two members are appointed by the President. Each of the six voting members of the commission must be confirmed by the majority of both Houses of Congress,

and each of the three appointing authorities is forbidden to choose both of their appointees from the same political party. . . .

A. Ripeness

. . . [I]n order to decide the basic question of whether the Act's provision for appointment of the members of the Commission violates the Constitution, we believe we are warranted in considering all of those aspects of the Commission's authority which have been presented by [the Court of Appeals' certified questions although many of the Commission's functions have not yet been exercised]. . . .

B. The Merits

Appellants urge that since Congress has given the Commission wideranging rule-making and enforcement powers with respect to the substantive provisions of the Act, Congress is precluded under the principle of separation of powers from vesting in itself the authority to appoint those who will exercise such authority. Their argument is based on the language of Art. II, § 2, cl. 2, of the Constitution, which provides in pertinent part as follows:

> "[The President] shall nominate, and by and with the Advice and Consent of the Senate, shall appoint . . . all other Officers of the United States, whose Appointments are not herein otherwise provided for, and which shall be established by Law: but the Congress may by Law vest the Appointment of such inferior Officers, as they think proper, in the President alone, in the Courts of Law, or in the Heads of Departments."

Appellants' argument is that this provision is the exclusive method by which those charged with executing the laws of the United States may be chosen. Congress, they assert, cannot have it both ways. If the legislature wishes the Commission to exercise all of the conferred powers, then its members are in fact "Officers of the United States" and must be appointed under the Appointments Clause. But if Congress insists upon retaining the power to appoint, then the members of the Commission may not discharge those many functions of the Commission which can be performed only by "Officers of the United States," as that term must be construed within the doctrine of separation of powers.

Appellee Federal Election Commission and *amici* in support of the Commission urge that the Framers of the Constitution, while mindful of the need for checks and balances among the three branches of the National Government, had no intention of denying to the Legislative Branch authority to appoint its own officers. Congress, either under the Appointments Clause or under its grants of substantive legislative authority and the Necessary and Proper Clause in Art. I, is in their view empowered to provide for the appointment to the Commission in the manner which it did because the Commission is performing "appropriate legislative functions.". . .

1. Separation of Powers

. . . Our inquiry of necessity touches upon the fundamental principles of the Government established by the Framers of the Constitution, and all litigants and all of the courts which have addressed themselves to the matter start on common ground in the recognition of the intent of the Framers that the powers of the three great branches of the National Government be largely separate from one another.

James Madison, writing in the Federalist No. 47, defended the work of the Framers against the charge that these three governmental powers were not *entirely* separate from one another in the proposed Constitution. . . .

Yet it is also clear from the provisions of the Constitution itself, and from the Federalist Papers, that the Constitution by no means contemplates total separation of each of these three essential branches of Government. The President is a participant in the law-making process by virtue of his

authority to veto bills enacted by Congress. The Senate is a participant in the appointive process by virtue of its authority to refuse to confirm persons nominated to office by the President. . . .

. . . Mr. Justice Jackson, concurring in the opinion and the judgment of the Court in *Youngstown Co. v. Sawyer* . . . (1952), succinctly characterized this understanding:

> "While the Constitution diffuses power the better to secure liberty, it also contemplates that practice will integrate the dispersed powers into a workable government. It enjoins upon its branches separateness but interdependence, autonomy but reciprocity."

The Framers regarded the checks and balances that they had built into the tripartite Federal Government as a self-executing safeguard against the encroachment or aggrandizement of one branch at the expense of the other. . . .

2. The Appointments Clause

The principle of separation of powers was not simply an abstract generalization in the minds of the Framers: it was woven into the document that they drafted in Philadelphia in the summer of 1787. Article I declares: "All legislative Powers herein granted shall be vested in a Congress of the United States." Article II vests the executive power "in a President of the United States of America," and Art. III declares that "the judicial Power of the United States, shall be vested in one supreme Court, and in such inferior Courts as the Congress may from time to time ordain and establish." The further concern of the Framers of the Constitution with maintenance of the separation of powers is found in the so-called "Ineligibility" and "Incompatibility" Clauses contained in § 6 of Art. I:

> "No Senator or Representative shall, during the Time for which he was elected, be appointed to any civil Office under the Authority of the United States, which shall have been created, or the Emoluments whereof shall have been increased during such time; and no Per-

son holding any Office under the United States, shall be a Member of either House during his Continuance in Office."

It is in the context of these cognate provisions of the document that we must examine the language of Art. II, § 2, cl. 2, which appellants contend provides the only authorization for appointment of those to whom substantial executive or administrative authority is given by statute. . . . [W]e again set out the provision:

> "[The President] shall nominate, and by and with the Advice and Consent of the Senate, shall appoint Ambassadors, other Public Ministers and Consuls, Judges of the supreme Court, and all other Officers of the United States, whose Appointments are not herein otherwise provided for, and which shall be established by Law, but the Congress may by Law vest the Appointment of such inferior Officers, as they think proper, in the President alone, in the Courts of Law, or in the Heads of Departments. . . .

. . . We think that the term "Officers of the United States" as used in Art. II . . . is a term intended to have substantive meaning. We think its fair import is that any appointee exercising significant authority pursuant to the laws of the United States is an Officer of the United States, and must, therefore, be appointed in the manner prescribed by § 2, cl. 2 of that Article.

If "all persons who can be said to hold an office under the government about to be established under the Constitution were intended to be included within one or the other of these modes of appointment," *United States v. Germaine,* [1878] it is difficult to see how the members of the Commission may escape inclusion. . . .

Although two members of the Commission are initially selected by the President, his nominations are subject to confirmation not merely by the Senate, but by the House of Representatives as well. The remaining four voting members of the Commission were appointed by the President *pro tempore* of the Senate and by the Speaker of the House. While the second part of the Clause authorizes Congress to vest the appointment of the officers described in that part in "the Courts of Law, or in the Heads of Departments," neither the Speaker of the House nor the President *pro tempore* of the Senate comes within this language.

. . . Thus with respect to four of the six voting members of the Commission, neither the President, the head of any department, nor the judiciary has any voice in their selection.

. . . Appellee commission and *amici* contend somewhat obliquely that because the Framers had no intention of relegating Congress to a position below that of the coequal Judicial and Executive Branches of the National Government, the Appointments Clause must somehow be read to include Congress or its officers as among those in whom the appointment power may be vested. But . . . the evolution of the draft version of the Constitution, seem[s] to us to lend considerable support to our reading of the language of the Appointments Clause itself.

An interim version of the draft Constitution had vested in the Senate the authority to appoint Ambassadors, public Ministers, and Judges of the Supreme Court, and the language of Art. II as finally adopted is a distinct change in this regard. We believe that it was a deliberate change made by the Framers with the intent to deny Congress any authority itself to appoint those who were "Officers of the United States.". . .

. . . Appellee Commission and *amici* urge that because of what they conceive to be the extraordinary authority reposed in Congress to regulate elections, this case stands on a different footing than if Congress had exercised its legislative authority in another field. . . . We see no reason to believe that the authority of Congress over federal election practices is of such a wholly different nature from the other grants of authority to Congress that it may be employed in such a manner as to offend well established constitutional restrictions stemming from the separation of powers.

The position that because Congress has been given explicit and plenary authority to regulate a field of activity, it must therefore have the power to appoint those who are to administer the regulatory statute is both novel and contrary to the language of the Appointments Clause. Unless their selection is elsewhere provided for, *all* officers of the United States are to be appointed in accordance with the Clause. . . . No class or type of officer is excluded because of its special functions. . . .

. . . We are also told by appellees and *amici* that Congress had good reason for not vesting in a Commission composed wholly of Presidential appointees the authority to administer the Act, since the administration of the Act would undoubtedly have a bearing on any incumbent President's campaign for re-election. . . . [I]t would seem that those who sought to challenge incumbent Congressmen might have equally good reason to fear a Commission which was unduly responsive to Members of Congress whom they were seeking to unseat. But such fears, however rational, do not by themselves warrant a distortion of the Framers' work.

Appellee Commission and *amici* finally contend . . . that whatever shortcomings the provisions of the appointment of members of the Commission might have under Art. II, Congress had ample authority under the Necessary and Proper Clause of Art. I to effectuate this result. We do not agree. The proper inquiry when considering the Necessary and Proper Clause is not the authority of Congress to create an office or a commission . . . but rather its authority to provide that its own officers may appoint to such office or commission.

. . . [Congress may not] vest in itself, or in its officers, the authority to appoint officers of the United States when the Appointments Clause by clear implication prohibits it from doing so. . . .

3. The Commission's Powers

Thus, on the assumption that all of the powers granted in the statute may be exercised by an agency whose members *have been* appointed in accordance with the Appointments Clause, the ultimate question in which, if any, of those powers may be exercised by the present Commissioners, none of whom *was* appointed as provided by that Clause. . . .

Insofar as the powers confided in the Commission are essentially of an investigative and informative nature, falling in the same general category as those powers which Congress might delegate to one of its own committees, there can be no question that the Commission as presently constituted may exercise them. . . .

But when we go beyond this type of authority to the more substantial powers exercised by the Commission, we reach a different result. The Commission's enforcement power, exemplified by its discretionary power to seek judicial relief, is authority that cannot possibly be regarded as merely in aid of the legislative function of Congress. A law suit is the ultimate remedy for a breach of the law, and it is to the President, and not to the Congress, that the Constitution entrusts the responsibility to "take Care that the Laws be faithfully executed." Art. II, § 3.

Congress may undoubtedly under the Necessary and Proper Clause create "offices" in the generic sense and provide such method of appointment to those "offices" as it chooses. But Congress' power under that Clause is inevitably bounded by the express language of Art. II, § 2, cl. 2, and unless the method it provides comports with the latter, the holders of those offices will not be "Officers of the United States." They may, therefore, properly perform duties only in aid of those functions that Congress may carry out by itself, or in an area sufficiently removed from the administration and enforcement of the public law as to permit them being performed by persons not "Officers of the United States.". . .

. . . We hold that these provisions of the Act, vesting in the Commission primary responsibility for conducting civil litigation in the courts of the United States for vindicating public rights, violate Art. II, cl 2, § 2, of the Constitution. Such functions may be discharged only by persons who are "Officers of the United States" within the language of that section.

All aspects of the Act are brought within the Commission's broad administrative powers: rule-making, advisory opinions, and determinations of eligibility for funds and even for federal elective office itself. These functions, exercised free from day-to-day supervision of either Congress or the Executive Branch, are more legislative and judicial in nature than are the Commission's enforcement powers, and are of kinds usually performed by independent regulatory agencies or by some department in the Executive Branch under the direction of an Act of Congress. Congress viewed these broad powers as essential to effective and impartial administration of the entire substantive framework of the Act. Yet each of these functions also represents the performance of a significant governmental duty exercised pursuant to a public law. . . . [N]one of them operates merely in aid of congressional authority to legislate or is sufficiently removed from the administration and enforcement of public law to allow it to be performed by the present Commission. These administrative functions may therefore be exercised only by persons who are "Officers of the United States."

It is also our view that the Commission's inability to exercise certain powers because of the method by which its members have been selected should not affect the validity of the Commission's administrative actions and determinations to this date, including its administration of those provisions, upheld today, authorizing the public financing of federal elections. The past acts of the Commission are therefore added *de facto* validity, just as we have recognized should be the case with respect to legislative acts performed by legislators held to have been elected in accordance with an unconstitutional apportionment plan. . . . We also draw on the Court's practice in the apportionment and voting rights cases and stay, for a period not to exceed 30 days, the Court's judgment insofar as it affects the authority of the Commission to exercise the duties and powers granted it under the Act. This limited stay will afford Congress an opportunity to reconstitute the Commission by law or to adopt other valid enforcement mechanisms without interrupting enforcement of the provisions the Court sustains, allowing the present Commission in the interim to function *de facto* in accordance with the substantive provisions of the Act. . . .

CONCLUSION

In summary, we sustain the individual contribution limits, the disclosure and reporting provisions, and the public financing scheme. We conclude, however, that the limitations on campaign expenditures, on independent expenditures by individuals and groups, and on expenditures by a candidate from his personal funds are constitutionally infirm. Finally, we hold that most of the powers conferred by the Act upon the Federal Election Commission can be exercised only by "Officers of the United States," appointed in conformity with Art. II, § 2, cl. 2, of the Constitution, and therefore cannot be exercised by the Commission as presently constituted.

In No. 75-436, the judgment of the Court of Appeals is affirmed in part and reversed in part. The judgment of the District Court in No. 75-437 is affirmed. The mandate shall issue forthwith, except that our judgment is stayed, for a period not to exceed 30 days, insofar as it affects the authority of the Commission to exercise the duties and powers granted it under the Act.

So ordered.

MR. CHIEF JUSTICE BURGER, concurring in part and dissenting in part.

For reasons set forth more fully later, I dissent from those parts of the Court's holding sustaining the Act's provisions (a) for disclosure of small contributions, (b) for limitations on contributions, and (c) for public financing of Presidential campaigns. In my view, the Act's disclosure scheme is impermissibly broad and violative of the First Amendment liberties and suffer from the same infirmities that the Court correctly sees in the expenditure ceilings. The Act's system for public financing of Presidential campaigns is, in my judgment, an impermissible intrusion by the Government into the traditionally private political process. . . .

DISCLOSURE PROVISIONS

Disclosure is, in principle, the salutary and constitutional remedy for most of the ills Congress was seeking to alleviate. I therefore agree fully with the broad proposition that public disclosure of contributions by individuals and by entities — particularly corporations and labor unions — is an effective means of revealing the type of political support that is sometimes coupled with expectations of special favors or rewards. That disclosure impinges on First Amendment rights is conceded by the Court . . . but given the objectives to which disclosure is directed, I agree that the need for disclosure outweighs individual constitutional claims. . . .

. . . The Court's theory, however, goes beyond permissible limits. Under the Court's view, disclosure serves broad informational purposes, enabling the public to be fully informed on matters of acute public interest. Forced disclosure of one aspect of a citizen's political activity, under this analysis, serves the public right-to-know. This open-ended approach is the only plausible justification for the otherwise irrationally low ceilings of $10 and $100 for anonymous contributions. The burdens of these low ceilings seem to me obvious, and the court does not try to question this. . . .

. . . The public right-to-know ought not be absolute when its exercise reveals private political convictions. Secrecy, like privacy, is not *per se* criminal. On the contrary, secrecy and privacy as to political preferences and convictions are fundamental in a free society. . . .

. . . With respect, I suggest the Court has failed to give the traditional standing to some of the First Amendment values at stake here. Specifically, it has failed to confine the particular exercise of governmental power within limits reasonably required. . . .

. . . [I]t seems to me that the threshold limits fixed at $10 and $100 for anonymous contributions are constitutionally impermissible on their face. . . . To argue that a 1976 contribution of $10 or $100 entails a risk of corruption or its appearance is simply too extravagant to be maintained. No public right-to-know justifies the compelled disclosure of such contributions, at the risk of discouraging them. There is, in short, no relation whatever between the means used and the legitimate goal of ventilating possible undue influence. Congress has used a shotgun to kill wrens as well as hawks. . . .

. . . Finally, no legitimate public interest has been shown in forcing the disclosure of modest contributions that are the prime support of new, unpopular or unfashionable political causes. There is no realistic possibility that such modest donations will have a corrupting influence especially on parties that enjoy only "minor" status. Major parties would not notice them, minor parties need them. . . .

I would therefore hold unconstitutional the provisions requiring reporting of contributions of $10 or more and to make a public record of the name, address, and occupation of a contributor of $100 or more.

CONTRIBUTION AND EXPENDITURE LIMITS

I agree fully with that part of the Court's opinion that holds unconstitutional the limitations the Act puts on campaign expenditures which "place substantial and direct restrictions on the ability of candidates, citizens, and associations to engage in protected political expression, restrictions that the First Amendment cannot tolerate." . . . Yet when it approves similarly stringent limitations on contributions, the Court ignores the reasons it finds so persuasive in the context of expenditures. For me contributions and expenditures are two sides of the same First Amendment coin. . . .

. . . The Court's attempt to distinguish the communication inherent in political *contributions* from the speech aspects of political *expenditures* simply will not wash. We do little but engage in word games unless we recognize that people — candidates and contributors — spend money on political activity because they wish to communicate ideas, and their constitutional interest in doing so is precisely the same whether they or someone else utter the words.

The Court attempts to make the Act seem less restrictive by casting the problem as one that goes to freedom of association rather than freedom of speech. I have long thought freedom of association and freedom of expression were two peas from the same pod. . . .

PUBLIC FINANCING

I dissent from Part III sustaining the constitutionality of the public financing provisions of the Act. . . .

. . . I would . . . fault the Court for not adequately analyzing and meeting head-on the issue whether public financial assistance to the private political activity of individual citizens and parties is a legitimate expenditure of public funds. The public monies at issue here are not being employed simply to police the integrity of the electoral process or to provide a forum for the use of all participants in the political dialog, as would, for example, be the case if free broadcast time were granted. Rather, we are confronted with the Government's actual financing, out of general revenues, a segment of the political debate itself. . . .

. . . I agree with MR. JUSTICE REHNQUIST that the scheme approved by the Court today invidiously discriminates against minor parties. . . . The fact that there have been few drastic realignments in our basic two-party structure in 200 years is no constitutional justification for freezing the status quo of the present major parties at the expense of such future political movements. . . .

I would also find unconstitutional the system of "matching grants" which makes a candidate's abil-

ity to amass private funds the sole criterion for eligibility for public funds. Such an arrangement can put at serious disadvantage a candidate with a potentially large, widely diffused — but poor — constituency. The ability of a candidate's supporters to help pay for his campaign cannot be equated with their willingness to cast a ballot for him. . . .

I cannot join in the attempt to determine which parts of the Act can survive review here. The statute as it now stands is unworkable and inequitable.

I agree with the Court's holding that the Act's restrictions on expenditures made "relative to a clearly identified candidate," independent of any candidate or his committee, are unconstitutional. . . . Paradoxically the Court upholds the limitations on individual contributions, which embrace precisely the same sort of expenditures "relative to a clearly identified candidate" if those expenditures are "authorized or requested" by the "candidate or his agents." . . . The Act as cut back by the Court thus places intolerable pressure on the distinction between "authorized" and "unauthorized" expenditures on behalf of a candidate; even those with the most sanguine hopes for the Act might well concede that the distinction cannot be maintained. . . .

. . . . Moreover, the Act — or so much as the Court leaves standing — creates significant inequities. A candidate with substantial personal resources is now given by the Court a clear advantage over his less affluent opponents, who are constrained by law in fundraising, because the Court holds that the "First Amendment cannot tolerate" any restrictions on spending. . . . Minority parties, whose situation is difficult enough under an Act that excludes them from public funding, are prevented from accepting large single-donor contributions. At the same time the Court sustains the provision aimed at broadening the base of political support by requiring candidates to seek a greater number of small contributors, it sustains the unrealistic disclosure thresholds of $10 and $100 that I believe will deter those hoped-for small contributions. Minor parties must now compete for votes against two major parties whose expenditures will be vast. Finally, the Act's distinction between contributions in money and contributions in services remains, with only the former being subject to any limits. . . .

The Court's piecemeal approach fails to give adequate consideration to the integrated nature of this legislation. A serious question is raised, which the court does not consider, when central segments, key operative provisions, of this Act are stricken, can what remains function in anything like the way Congress intended? . . .

Finally, I agree with the Court that members of the Federal Election Commission were unconstitutionally appointed. However, I disagree that we should give blanket *de facto* validation to all actions of the Commission undertaken until today. . . .

. . . In my view Congress can no more ration political expression than it can ration religious expression; and limits on political or religious contributions and expenditures effectively curb expression in both areas. There are many prices we pay for the freedoms secured by the First Amendment; the risk of undue influence is one of them, confirming what we have long known: freedom is hazardous, but some restraints are worse.

MR. JUSTICE WHITE, concurring in part and dissenting in part. . . .

[I]

. . . The disclosure requirements and the limitations and expenditures are challenged as invalid abridgements of the right of free speech protected by the First Amendment. I would reject these challenges. I agree with the Court's conclusion and much of its opinion with respect to sustaining the disclosure provisions. I am also in agreement with the Court's judgment upholding the limitations on contributions. I dissent, however, from the Court's view that the expenditure limitations of 18 U.S.C. §§ 608 (c) and (e) violate the First Amendment. . . .

. . . Since the contribution and expenditure limitations are neutral as to the content of speech and

are not motivated by fear of the consequences of the political speech of particular candidates or of political speech in general, this case depends on whether the nonspeech interests of the Federal Government in regulating the use of money in political campaigns are sufficiently urgent to justify the incidental effects that the limitations visit upon the First Amendment interests of candidates and their supporters. . . .

. . . It would make little sense to me, and apparently made none to Congress, to limit the amounts an individual may give to a candidate or spend with his approval but fail to limit the amounts that could be spent on his behalf. Yet the Court permits the former while striking down the later limitation. . . .

. . . Proceeding from the maxim that "money talks," the Court finds that the expenditure limitations will seriously curtail political expression by candidates and interfere substantially with their chances for election. . . .

. . . [A]s it should be unnecessary to point out, money is not always equivalent to or used for speech, even in the context of political campaigns. I accept the reality that communicating with potential voters is the heart of an election campaign and that widespread communication has become very expensive. There are, however, many expensive campaign activities that are not themselves communicative or remotely related to speech. Furthermore, campaigns differ among themselves. Some seem to spend much less money than others and yet communicate as much or more than those supported by enormous bureaucracies with unlimited financing. The record before us no more supports the conclusion that the communicative efforts of congressional and Presidential candidates will be crippled by the expenditure limitations than it supports the contrary. The judgment of Congress was that reasonably effective campaigns could be conducted within the limits established by the Act and that the communicative efforts of these campaigns would not seriously suffer. In this posture of the case, there is no sound basis for invalidating the expenditure limitations, so long as the purposes they serve are legitimate and sufficiently substantial, which in my view they are. . . .

. . . It is also important to restore and maintain public confidence in federal elections. It is critical to obviate or dispel the impression that federal elections are purely and simply a function of money, that federal offices are bought and sold or that political races are reserved for those who have the facility — and the stomach — for doing whatever it takes to bring together those interests, groups, and individuals that can raise or contribute large fortunes in order to prevail at the polls.

The ceiling on candidate expenditures represents the considered judgment of Congress that elections are to be decided among candidates none of whom has overpowering advantage by reason of a huge campaign war chest. At least so long as the ceiling placed upon the candidates is not plainly too low, elections are not to turn on the difference in the amounts of money that candidates have to spend. This seems an acceptable purpose and the means chosen a common sense way to achieve it. The Court nevertheless holds that a candidate has a constitutional right to spend unlimited amounts of money, mostly that of other people, in order to be elected. The holding perhaps is not that federal candidates have the constitutional right to purchase their election, but many will so interpret the Court's conclusion in this case. I cannot join the Court in this respect.

I also disagree with the Court's judgment that § 608 (a), which limits the amount of money that a candidate or his family may spend on his campaign, violates the Constitution. Although it is true that this provision does not promote any interest in preventing the corruption of candidates, the provision does, nevertheless, serve salutary purposes related to the integrity of federal campaigns. . . .

As with the campaign expenditure limits, Congress was entitled to determine that personal wealth ought to play a less important role in political campaigns than it has in the past. Nothing in the First Amendment stands in the way of that determination. . . .

[II]

I join the answers in Part IV of the Court's opinion . . . to the questions certified by the District Court relating to the composition and powers of the Federal Election Commission (FEC). . . .

. . . It is apparent that none of the members of the FEC is selected in a manner Art. II specifies for the appointment of officers of the United States. . . .

. . . The challenge to the FEC, therefore, is that its members are officers of the United States the mode of whose appointment was required to, but did not, conform to the Appointments Clause. That challenge is well taken. . . .

. . . This position that Congress may itself appoint the members of a body that is to administer a wide-ranging statute will not withstand examination in light of either the purpose and history of the Appointments Clause or of prior cases in this Court. . . .

. . . I thus find singularly unpersuasive the proposition that because the FEC is implementing statutory policies with respect to the conduct of elections, which policies Congress has the power to propound, its members may be appointed by Congress. One might as well argue that the exclusive and plenary power of Congress over interstate commerce authorizes Congress to appoint the members of the Interstate Commerce Commission and of many other regulatory commissions. . . .

. . . Congress clearly has the power to create federal offices and to define the powers and duties of those offices . . . but no case in this Court even remotely supports the power of Congress to appoint an officer of the United States aside from those officers each House is authorized by Art. I to appoint to assist in the legislative processes. . . .

MR. JUSTICE MARSHALL, concurring in part and dissenting in part.

I join in all of the Court's opinion except Part I - C - 2, which deals with § 608 (a) of the Act. That section limits the amount a candidate can spend from his personal funds, or family funds under his control, in connection with his campaigns during any calendar year. . . .

. . . One of the points on which all Members of the Court agree is that money is essential for effective communication in a political campaign. It would appear to follow that the candidate with a substantial personal fortune at his disposal is off to a significant "head start." Of course, the less wealthy candidate can potentially overcome the disparity in resources through contributions from others. But ability to generate contributions may itself depend upon a showing of a financial base for the campaign or some demonstration of pre-existing support, which in turn is facilitated by expenditures of substantial personal sums. Thus the wealthy candidate's immediate access to a substantial personal fortune may give him an initial advantage that his less wealthy opponent can never overcome. And even if the advantage can be overcome, the perception that personal wealth wins elections may not only discourage potential candidates without significant personal wealth from entering the political arena, but also undermine public confidence in the integrity of the electoral process. . . .

. . . In view of § 608 (b)'s limitations on contributions, then, § 608 (a) emerges not simply as a device to reduce the natural advantage of the wealthy candidate, but as a provision providing some symmetry to a regulatory scheme that otherwise enhances the natural advantage of the wealthy. . . . I therefore respectfully dissent from the Court's invalidation of § 608 (a).

MR. JUSTICE BLACKMUN, concurring in part and dissenting in part.

I am not persuaded that the Court makes, or indeed is able to make, a principled constitutional distinction between the contribution limitations, on the one hand, and the expenditure limitations, on the other, that are involved here. I therefore do not join in Part I-B of the Court's opinion or those portions of Part I-A that are consistent with Part I-B. As to those, I dissent. . . .

MR. JUSTICE REHNQUIST, concurring in part and dissenting in part. . . .

. . . I . . . join in all of the Court's opinion except Subpart III-B-1, which sustains, against appellants' First and Fifth Amendment challenges, the disparities found in the congressional plan for financing general Presidential elections between the two major parties, on the one hand, and minor parties and candidacies on the other. . . .

. . . Congress, of course, does have an interest in not "funding hopeless candidacies with large sums of public money," . . . and many for that purpose legitimately require " 'some preliminary showing of a significant modicum of support,' *Jenness v. Fortson* . . . as an eligibility requirement for public funds." . . . But Congress in this legislation has done a good deal more than that. It has enshrined the Republican and Democratic Parties in a permanently preferred position, and has established requirements for funding minor party and independent candidates to which the two major parties are not subject. Congress would undoubtedly be justified in treating the Presidential candidates of the two major parties differently from minor party or independent Presidential candidates, in view of the long demonstrated public supports of the former. But because of the First Amendment overtones of the appellants' Fifth Amendment equal protection claim, something more than a merely rational basis for the difference in treatment must be shown, as the Court apparently recognizes. I find it impossible to subscribe to the Court's reasoning that because no third party has posed a credible threat to the two major parties in Presidential elections since 1860, Congress may by law attempt to assure that this pattern will endure forever.

I would hold that, as to general election financing, Congress has not merely treated the two major parties differently from minor parties and independents, but has discriminated in favor of the former in such a way as to run afoul of the Fifth and First Amendments to the United States Constitution.

FEDERAL ELECTION CAMPAIGN ACT OF 1971

The Federal Election Campaign Act of 1971 (P.L. 92-225) was the first comprehensive revision of federal campaign legislation since the Corrupt Practices Act of 1925. It established detailed spending limits and disclosure procedures. The act contained the following major provisions, some of which have been declared unconstitutional and others superseded by later amendments or repealed:

General

- Repealed the Federal Corrupt Practices Act of 1925.
- Defined "election" to mean any general, special, primary, or runoff election, nominating convention or caucus, delegate-selection primary, presidential preference primary, or constitutional convention.
- Broadened the definitions of "contribution" and "expenditure" as they pertain to political campaigns, but exempted a loan of money by a national or state bank made in accordance with applicable banking laws.
- Prohibited promises of employment or other political rewards or benefits by any candidate in exchange for political support, and prohibited contracts between candidates and any federal department or agency.
- Provided that the terms "contribution" and "expenditure" did not include communications, nonpartisan registration, and get-out-the-vote campaigns by a corporation aimed at its stockholders or by a labor organization aimed at its members.
- Provided that the terms "contribution" and "expenditure" did not include the establishment, administration, and solicitation of voluntary contributions to a separate segregated fund to be utilized for political purposes by a corporation or labor organization.

Contribution Limits

- Placed a ceiling on contributions by any candidate or his immediate family to his own campaign of $50,000 for president or vice president, $35,000 for senator, and $25,000 for representative.

Spending Limits

- Limited the total amount that could be spent by federal candidates for advertising time in communications media to 10 cents per eligible voter or $50,000, whichever was greater. The limitation would apply to all candidates for president and vice president, senator, and representative, and would be determined annually for the geographical area of each election by the Bureau of the Census.
- Included in the term "communications media" radio and television broadcasting stations, newspapers, magazines, billboards, and automatic telephone equipment. Of the total spending limit, up to 60 percent could be used for broadcast advertising time.
- Specified that candidates for presidential nomination, during the period prior to the nominating convention, could spend no more in primary or nonprimary states than the amount allowed under the 10-cent-per-voter communications spending limitation.
- Provided that broadcast and nonbroadcast spending limitations be increased in proportion to annual increases in the Consumer Price Index over the base year 1970.

Disclosure and Enforcement

- Required all political committees that anticipated receipts in excess of $1,000 during the calendar year to file a statement of organization with the appropriate federal supervisory

officer, and to include such information as the
names of all principal officers, the scope of the
committee, the names of all candidates the
committee supported, and other information as
required by law.

- Stipulated that the appropriate federal supervisory officer to oversee election campaign
practices, reporting, and disclosure was the
clerk of the House for House candidates, the
secretary of the Senate for Senate candidates,
and the Comptroller General for presidential
candidates.
- Required each political committee to report
any individual expenditure of more than $100
and any expenditures of more than $100 in
the aggregate during the calendar year.
- Required disclosure of all contributions to any
committee or candidate in excess of $100,
including a detailed report with the name and
address of the contributor and the date the
contribution was made.
- Required the supervisory officers to prepare
an annual report for each committee registered
with the Federal Election Commission (FEC)
and make such reports available for sale to the
public.
- Required candidates and committees to file
reports of contributions and expenditures on
the 10th day of March, June, and September
every year, on the 15th and 5th days preceding
the date on which an election was held, and on
the 31st day of January. Any contribution of
$5,000 or more was to be reported within
forty-eight hours after its receipt.
- Required reporting of the names, addresses,
and occupations of any lender and endorser of
any loan in excess of $100 as well as the date
and amount of such loans.
- Required any person who made any contribution in excess of $100, other than through a
political committee or candidate, to report such
contribution to the FEC.
- Prohibited any contribution to a candidate or
committee by one person in the name of
another person.

- Authorized the office of the comptroller general to serve as a national clearinghouse for
information on the administration of election
practices.
- Required that copies of reports filed by a
candidate with the appropriate supervisory
officer also be filed with the secretary of state
for the state in which the election was held.

Miscellaneous

- Prohibited radio and television stations from
charging political candidates more than the
lowest unit cost for the same advertising time
available to commercial advertisers. Lowest
unit rate charges would apply only during the
forty-five days preceding a primary election
and the sixty days preceding a general
election.
- Required nonbroadcast media to charge candidates no more than the comparable amounts
charged to commercial advertisers for the same
class and amount of advertising space. The
requirement would apply only during the
forty-five days preceding the date of a primary
election and sixty days before the date of a
general election.
- Provided that amounts spent by an agent of a
candidate on behalf of his candidacy would be
charged against the overall expenditure alloca-
tion. Fees paid to the agent for services performed also would be charged against the
overall limitation.
- Stipulated that no broadcast station could
make any charge for political advertising time
on a station unless written consent to contract
for such time had been given by the candidate,
and unless the candidate certified that such
charge would not exceed his spending limit.

THE REVENUE ACT OF 1971

The Revenue Act of 1971 (P.L. 92-178), through tax incentives and a tax checkoff plan, provided the basis for public funding of presidential election campaigns. The act contained the following major provisions, some of which have been declared unconstitutional and others superseded by later amendments or repealed:

Tax Incentives and Checkoff

- Allowed a tax credit of $12.50 ($25 for a married couple) or a deduction against income of $50 ($100 for a married couple) for political contributions to candidates for local, state, or federal office.
- Allowed taxpayers to contribute to a general fund for all eligible presidential and vice presidential candidates by authorizing $1 of their annual income tax payment to be placed in such a fund.

Presidential Election Campaign Fund

- Authorized to be distributed to the candidates of each major party (one which obtained 25 percent of votes cast in the previous presidential election) an amount equal to 15 cents multiplied by the number of U.S. residents age eighteen or over.
- Established a formula for allocating public campaign funds to candidates of minor parties whose candidates received 5 percent or more but less than 25 percent of the previous presidential election vote.
- Authorized payments after the election to reimburse the campaign expenses of a new party whose candidate received enough votes to be eligible or to a minor party whose candidate increased its vote to the qualifying level.
- Prohibited major-party candidates who chose public financing of their campaign from accepting private campaign contributions unless their share of funds contributed through the income tax checkoff procedure fell short of the amounts to which they were entitled.
- Prohibited major-party candidates who chose public financing and all campaign committees authorized by candidates from spending more than the amount to which the candidates were entitled under the contributions formula.
- Provided that if the amounts in the fund were insufficient to make the payments to which each party was entitled, payments would be allocated according to the ratio of contributions in their accounts. No party would receive from the general fund more than the smallest amount needed by a major party to reach the maximum amount of contributions to which it was entitled.
- Provided that surpluses remaining in the fund after a campaign be returned to the Treasury after all parties had been paid the amounts to which they were entitled.

Enforcement

- Provided penalties of $5,000 or one year in prison, or both, for candidates or campaign committees that spent more on a campaign than the amounts they received from the campaign fund or who accepted private contributions when sufficient public funds were available.
- Provided penalties of $10,000 or five years in prison, or both, for candidates or campaign committees who used public campaign funds for unauthorized expenses, gave or accepted kickbacks or illegal payments involving public campaign funds, or who knowingly furnished false information to the comptroller general.

FEDERAL ELECTION CAMPAIGN ACT AMENDMENTS OF 1974

The Federal Election Campaign Act Amendments of 1974 (P.L. 93-443) set new contribution and spending limits, made provision for government funding of presidential prenomination campaigns and national nominating conventions, and created the bipartisan Federal Election Commission to administer election laws. The law contained the following major provisions, some of which have been declared unconstitutional and others superseded by later amendments or repealed:

Federal Election Commission

- Created a six-member, full-time bipartisan Federal Election Commission (FEC) to be responsible for administering election laws and the public financing program.
- Provided that the president, speaker of the House, and president pro tem of the Senate would appoint to the FEC two members, each of different parties, all subject to confirmation by Congress. Commission members could not be officials or employees of any branch of government.
- Made the secretary of the Senate and clerk of the House ex officio, nonvoting members of the FEC; provided that their offices would serve as custodian of reports for House and Senate candidates.
- Provided that commissioners would serve six-year, staggered terms and established a rotating one-year chairmanship.

Contribution Limits

- $1,000 per individual for each primary, run-off, or general election, and an aggregate contribution of $25,000 to all federal candidates annually.
- $5,000 per organization, political committee, and national and state party organization for each election, but no aggregate limit on the amount organizations could contribute in a campaign nor on the amount organizations could contribute to party organizations supporting federal candidates.
- $50,000 for president or vice president, $35,000 for Senate, and $25,000 for House races for candidates and their families to their own campaign.
- $1,000 for independent expenditures on behalf of a candidate.
- Barred cash contributions of over $100 and foreign contributions.

Spending Limits

- Presidential primaries—$10 million total per candidate for all primaries. In a state presidential primary, limited a candidate to spending no more than twice what a Senate candidate in that state would be allowed to spend.
- Presidential general election—$20 million per candidate.
- Presidential nominating conventions—$2 million each major political party, lesser amounts for minor parties.
- Senate primaries—$100,000 or eight cents per eligible voter, whichever was greater.
- Senate general elections—$150,000 or twelve cents per eligible voter, whichever was greater.
- House primaries—$70,000.
- House general elections—$70,000.
- National party spending—$10,000 per candidate in House general elections; $20,000 or two cents per eligible voter, whichever was greater, for each candidate in Senate general elections; and two cents per voter (approximately $2.9 million) in presidential general elections. The expenditure would be above the candidate's individual spending limit.
- Applied Senate spending limits to House can-

didates who represented a whole state.

- Repealed the media spending limitations in the Federal Election Campaign Act of 1971 (P.L. 92-225).
- Exempted expenditures of up to $500 for food and beverages, invitations, unreimbursed travel expenses by volunteers, and spending on "slate cards" and sample ballots.
- Exempted fund-raising costs of up to 20 percent of the candidate spending limit. Thus thespending limit for House candidates would beeffectively raised from $70,000 to $84,000 and for candidates in presidential primaries from $10 million to $12 million.
- Provided that spending limits be increased in proportion to annual increases in the Consumer Price Index.

Public Financing

- Presidential general elections—voluntary public financing. Major party candidates automatically would qualify for full funding before the campaign. Minor party and independent candidates would be eligible to receive a proportion of full funding based on past or current votes received. If a candidate opted for full public funding, no private contributions would be permitted.
- Presidential nominating conventions—optional public funding. Major parties automatically would qualify. Minor parties would be eligible for lesser amounts based on their proportion of votes received in a past election.
- Presidential primaries—matching public funds of up to $5 million per candidate after meeting fund-raising requirements of $100,000 raised in amounts of at least $5,000 in each of twenty states or more. Only the first $250 of individual private contributions would be matched. The matching funds were to be divided among the candidates as quickly as possible. In allocating the money, the order in which the candidates qualified would be taken into account. Only private gifts, raised after

January 1, 1975, would qualify for matching for the 1976 election. No federal payments would be made before January 1976.

- Provided that all federal money for public funding of campaigns would come from the Presidential Election Campaign Fund. Money received from the federal income tax dollar checkoff automatically would be appropriated to the fund.

Disclosure and Enforcement

- Required each candidate to establish one central campaign committee through which all contributions and expenditures on behalf of a candidate must be reported. Required designation of specific bank depositories of campaign funds.
- Required full reports of contributions and expenditures to be filed with the FEC ten days before and thirty days after every election, and within ten days of the close of each quarter unless the committee received or expended less than $1,000 in that quarter. A year-end report was due in nonelection years.
- Required that contributions of $1,000 or more received within the last fifteen days before election be reported to the FEC within forty-eight hours.
- Prohibited contributions in the name of another.
- Treated loans as contributions. Required a cosigner or guarantor for each $1,000 of outstanding obligation.
- Required any organization that spent any money or committed any act for the purpose of influencing any election (such as the publication of voting records) to file reports as a political committee.
- Required every person who spent or contributed more than $100, other than to or through a candidate or political committee, to report.
- Permitted government contractors, unions, and corporations to maintain separate, segregated political funds.

- Provided that the FEC would receive campaign reports, make rules and regulations (subject to review by Congress within thirty days), maintain a cumulative index of reports filed and not filed, make special and regular reports to Congress and the president, and serve as an election information clearinghouse.
- Gave the FEC power to render advisory opinions, conduct audits and investigations, subpoena witnesses and information, and go to court to seek civil injunctions.
- Provided that criminal cases would be referred by the FEC to the Justice Department for prosecution.
- Increased existing fines to a maximum of $50,000.
- Provided that a candidate for federal office who failed to file reports could be prohibited from running again for the term of that office plus one year.

Miscellaneous

- Set January 1, 1975, as the effective date of the act (except for immediate preemption of state laws).
- Removed Hatch Act restrictions on voluntary activities by state and local employees in federal campaigns, if not otherwise prohibited by state law.
- Prohibited solicitation of funds by franked mail.
- Preempted state election laws for federal candidates.
- Permitted use of excess campaign funds to defray expenses of holding federal office or for other lawful purposes.

FEDERAL ELECTION CAMPAIGN ACT AMENDMENTS OF 1976

The Federal Election Campaign Act Amendments of 1976 (P.L. 94-283) revised election laws following the Supreme Court decision in Buckley v. Valeo. *The amendments reopened the door to large contributions through "independent expenditures" and through corporate and union political action committees. The law contained the following major provisions, some of which have been superseded by later amendments or repealed:*

Federal Election Commission

- Reconstituted the Federal Election Commission (FEC) as a six-member panel appointed by the president and confirmed by the Senate.
- Prohibited FEC members from engaging in outside business activities; gave commissioners one year after joining the body to terminate outside business interests.
- Gave Congress the power to disapprove individual sections of any regulation proposed by the FEC.

Contribution Limits

- Limited an individual to giving no more than $5,000 a year to a political action committee (PAC) and $20,000 to the national committee of a political party (the 1974 law set a $1,000-per-election limit on individual contributions to a candidate and an aggregate contribution limit for individuals of $25,000 a year, both provisions remaining in effect).
- Limited a multicandidate committee to giving no more than $15,000 a year to the national committee of a political party (the 1974 law set only a limit of $5,000 per election per candidate, a provision remaining in effect).

- Limited the Democratic and Republican senatorial campaign committees to giving no more than $17,500 a year to a candidate (the 1974 law set a $5,000-per-election limit, a provision remaining in effect).
- Allowed campaign committees organized to back a single candidate to provide "occasional, isolated, and incidental support" to another candidate. (The 1974 law had limited such a committee to spending money only on behalf of the single candidate for which it was formed.)
- Restricted the proliferation of membership organization, corporate, and union PACs. All PACs established by a company or an international union would be treated as a single committee for contribution purposes. The contributions of PACs of a company or union would be limited to no more than $5,000 overall to the same candidate in any election.

Spending Limits

- Limited spending by presidential and vice presidential candidates to no more than $50,000 of their own, or their families', money on their campaigns, if they accepted public financing.
- Exempted from the law's spending limits payments by candidates or the national committees of political parties for legal and accounting services required to comply with the campaign law, but required that such payments be reported.

Public Financing

- Required presidential candidates who received federal matching subsidies and who withdrew from the prenomination election campaign to give back leftover federal matching funds.
- Cut off federal campaign subsidies to a presidential candidate who won less than 10 percent of the vote in two consecutive presidential primaries in which he ran.

- Established a procedure under which an individual who became ineligible for matching payments could have eligibility restored by a finding of the FEC.

Disclosure and Enforcement

- Gave the FEC exclusive authority to prosecute civil violations of the campaign finance law and shifted to the FEC jurisdiction over violations formerly covered only in the criminal code, thus strengthening its power to enforce the law.
- Required an affirmative vote of four members for the FEC to issue regulations and advisory opinions and initiate civil actions and investigations.
- Required labor unions, corporations, and membership organizations to report expenditures of over $2,000 per election for communications to their stockholders or members advocating the election or defeat of a clearly identified candidate. The costs of communications to members or stockholders on issues would not have to be reported.
- Required that candidates and political committees keep records of contributions of $50 or more. (The 1974 law had required records of contributions of $10 or more.)
- Permitted candidates and political committees to waive the requirement for filing quarterly campaign finance reports in a nonelection year if less than a total of $5,000 was raised or spent in that quarter. Annual reports would still have to be filed. (The exemption limit was $1,000 under the 1974 law.)
- Required political committees and individuals making an independent political expenditure of more than $100 that advocated the defeat or election of a candidate to file a report with the election commission. Required the committee and individual to state, under penalty of perjury, that the expenditure was not made in collusion with a candidate.
- Required that independent expenditures of $1,000 or more made within fifteen days of an

election be reported within twenty-four hours.

- Limited the FEC to issuing advisory opinions only for specific fact situations. Advisory opinions could not be used to spell out FEC policy. Advisory opinions were not to be considered as precedents unless an activity was "indistinguishable in all its material aspects" from an activity already covered by an advisory opinion.

- Permitted the FEC to initiate investigations only after it received a properly verified complaint or had reason to believe, based on information it obtained in the normal course of its duties, that a violation had occurred or was about to occur. The FEC was barred from relying on anonymous complaints to institute investigations.

- Required the FEC to rely initially on conciliation to deal with alleged campaign law violations before going to court. The FEC was allowed to refer alleged criminal violations to the Department of Justice for action. The attorney general was required to report back to the FEC within sixty days an action taken on the apparent violation and subsequently every thirty days until the matter was disposed of.

- Provided for a one-year jail sentence and a fine of up to $25,000 or three times the amount of the contribution or expenditure involved in the violation, whichever was greater, if an individual was convicted of knowingly committing a campaign law violation that involved more than $1,000.

- Provided for civil penalties of fines of $5,000 or an amount equal to the contribution or expenditure involved in the violation, whichever was greater. For violations knowingly committed, the fine would be $10,000 or an amount equal to twice the amount involved in the violation, whichever was greater. The fines could be imposed by the courts or by the commission in conciliation agreements. (The 1974 law included penalties for civil violations of a $1,000 fine and/or a one-year prison sentence.)

Miscellaneous

- Restricted the fund-raising ability of corporate PACs. Company committees could seek contributions only from stockholders and executive and administrative personnel and their families. Restricted union PACs to soliciting contributions only from union members and their families. However, twice a year the law permitted union and corporate PACs to seek campaign contributions only by mail from all employees not initially included in the restriction. Contributions would have to remain anonymous and would be received by an independent third party that would keep records but pass the money to the committees.

- Permitted trade association PACs to solicit contributions from member companies' stockholders, executive and administrative personnel, and their families.

- Permitted union PACs to use the same method to solicit campaign contributions that the PAC of the company uses. The union committee would have to reimburse the company at cost for the expenses the company incurred for the political fund raising.

FEDERAL ELECTION CAMPAIGN ACT AMENDMENTS OF 1979

The Federal Election Campaign Act Amendments of 1979 (P.L. 96-187) were enacted to lighten the burden the law imposed on candidates and political committees by reducing paperwork, among other changes. The law contained the following major provisions:

Disclosure

- Required a federal candidate to file campaign

finance reports if he or she received or expended more than $5,000. Previously any candidate, regardless of the amount raised or spent, had to file.

- Allowed local political party organizations to avoid filing reports with the Federal Election Commission (FEC) if expenditures for certain voluntary activities (get-out-the-vote and voter registration drives for presidential tickets and purchase of buttons, bumper stickers, and other materials) were less than $5,000 a year. If other types of expenditures were more than $1,000 a year, then such a group would be required to file. Previously local political party organizations were required to file when any class of expenditure exceeded $1,000 a year.
- Permitted an individual to spend up to $1,000 in behalf of a candidate or $2,000 in behalf of a political party in voluntary expenses for providing his home, food, or personal travel without its being counted as a reportable contribution.
- Eliminated the requirement that a political committee have a chairman, but continued the requirement that each have a treasurer.
- Allowed ten days, instead of the previous five, for a person who received a contribution of more than $50 on behalf of a candidate's campaign committee to forward it to the committee's treasurer.
- Required a committee's treasurer to preserve records for three years. Previously, the FEC established the period of time that committee treasurers were required to keep records.
- Required a candidate's campaign committee to have the candidate's name in the title of the committee. Also, the title of a political action committee (PAC) was required to include the name of the organization with which it was affiliated.
- Reduced to six from eleven the categories of information required on registration statements of political committees. One of the categories eliminated was one requiring PACs to name the candidates supported. That re-

quirement meant that PACs were forced frequently to file lists of candidates to whom they contributed when that information already was given in their contribution reports.

- Reduced to nine from twenty-four the maximum number of reports that a candidate would be required to file during a two-year election cycle. Those nine reports would be a pre-primary, a pre-general, a postgeneral, four quarterly reports during an election year, and two semiannual reports during the nonelection year. The preelection reports would be due twelve days before the election; the postgeneral report would be due thirty days after the election; the quarterly reports would be due fifteen days after the end of each quarter; and the semiannual reports would be due July 31 and January 31.
- Required presidential campaign committees to file monthly reports, as well as pre- and postgeneral reports, during an election year if they had contributions or expenditures in excess of $100,000. All other presidential campaign committees would be required to file quarterly reports, as well as pre- and postgeneral reports, during an election year. During a nonelection year presidential campaign committees could choose whether to file monthly or quarterly reports.
- Required political committees other than those affiliated with a candidate to file either monthly reports in all years or nine reports during a two-year election cycle.
- Provided that the FEC be notified within forty-eight hours of contributions of $1,000 or more that were made between twenty days and forty-eight hours before an election. Previously the period had been between fifteen days and forty-eight hours before an election.
- Required the names of contributors to be reported if they gave $200 or more instead of $100 or more.
- Required expenses to be itemized if they were $200 or more instead of $100 or more.
- Increased the threshold for reporting indepen-

dent expenditures to $250 from $100.

Federal Election Commission

- Established a "best effort" standard for the FEC to determine compliance by candidates' committees with the law. This was intended to ease the burden on committees, particularly in the area of meeting the requirement of filing the occupations of contributors.
- Allowed any person who had an inquiry about a specific campaign transaction—not just federal officeholders, candidates, political committees, and the national party committees—to request advisory opinions from the FEC.
- Required the FEC to respond to advisory opinion requests within sixty days instead of within a "reasonable time." If such a request were made within the sixty-day period before an election, the FEC would be required to issue an opinion within twenty days.
- Provided that within five days of receiving a complaint that the election campaign law had been violated the FEC must notify any person alleged to have committed a violation. The accused has fifteen days in which to respond to the complaint.
- Required a vote of four of the six members of the FEC to make the determination it had "reason to believe" a violation of the law had occurred. An investigation then would be required, and the accused had to be notified.
- Provided that four votes of the FEC were necessary to determine "probable cause" that a violation had occurred. The FEC then would be required to attempt to correct the violation by informal methods and to enter into a conciliation agreement within ninety days. Commission action required the vote of four FEC members.
- Narrowed the scope of the FEC's national clearinghouse function from all elections to federal elections.
- Eliminated random audits of committees by the FEC and required a vote of four FEC

members to conduct an audit after it had determined that a committee had not substantially complied with the election campaign law.
- Required secretaries of state in each state to keep copies of FEC reports on file for only two years compared with the previous requirement that all House candidate reports be retained for five years and all other reports for ten years.
- Provided an expedited procedure for the Senate, as well as for the House, to disapprove a regulation proposed by the FEC.

Enforcement

- Retained the substance of the existing law providing for civil and criminal relief of election campaign law violations.
- Continued the prohibition on the use of the contents of reports filed with the FEC for the purpose of soliciting contributions or for commercial purposes, but added the exception that the names of PACs registered with the FEC may be used for solicitation of contributions.
- Permitted political committees to include ten pseudonyms on each report to protect against illegal use of the names of contributors. A list of those names would be provided to the FEC and would not be made public.

Political Parties

- Allowed state and local party groups to buy, without limit, buttons, bumper stickers, handbills, brochures, posters, and yard signs for voluntary activities.
- Authorized state and local party groups to conduct voter registration and get-out-the-vote drives on behalf of presidential tickets without financial limit.

Public Financing

- Increased the allotment of federal funds for the

Democrats and Republicans to finance their nominating conventions to $3 million from $2 million.

Miscellaneous

- Permitted buttons and similar materials, but not commercial advertisements, that promoted one candidate to make a passing reference to another federal candidate without its being treated as a contribution to the second candidate.
- Permitted leftover campaign funds to be given to other political committees, as well as charities.
- Prohibited anyone, with the exception of members of Congress at the time of P.L. 96-187's enactment, to convert leftover campaign funds to personal use.

- Continued the ban on solicitation by candidates for Congress or members of Congress and by federal employees of other federal workers for campaign contributions, but dropped the prohibition on the receipt of such contributions by federal employees. An inadvertent solicitation of a federal employee would not be a violation.
- Permitted congressional employees to make voluntary contributions to members of Congress other than their immediate employers.
- Continued the ban on solicitation and receipt of contributions in a federal building. But it would not be a violation if contributions received at a federal building were forwarded within seven days to the appropriate political committee and if the contribution had not been directed initially to the federal building.

SELECTED READINGS

Adamany, David, and George E. Agree. *Political Money: A Strategy for Campaign Financing in America.* Baltimore: Johns Hopkins University Press, 1975.

Alexander, Herbert E. *Financing Politics: Money, Elections, and Political Reform.* 4th ed. Washington, D.C.: CQ Press, 1992.

Alexander, Herbert E., and Monica Bauer, *Financing the 1988 Election.* Boulder, Colo.: Westview Press, 1991. (Eighth in quadrennial series that began with the 1960 elections.)

Cantor, Joseph E. "Campaign Financing in Federal Elections: A Guide to the Law and Its Operation." Rept. No. 89-451 GOV. Congressional Research Service, Library of Congress, July 31, 1989.

——. "Political Action Committees: Their Evolution, Growth, and Implications for the Political System." Rept. No. 84-78 GOV. Congressional Research Service, Library of Congress, April 30, 1984. Addendum, April 21, 1986.

Cantor, Joseph E., and Kevin J. Coleman. "Expenditures for Campaign Services: A Survey of 1988 Congressional Candidates in Competitive Elections." Rept. No. 90-457 GOV. Congressional Research Service, Library of Congress, September 12, 1990. Addendum, November 8, 1990.

Center for Responsive Politics. *Campaign Spending Out of Control.* Washington, D.C., 1985.

——. *PACs on PACs: The View from the Inside.* Washington, D.C., 1988.

——. *Soft Money—A Loophole for the '80s.* Washington, D.C., 1985.

——. *Spending in Congressional Elections: A Never Ending Spiral.* Washington, D.C., 1988.

Dodd, Lawrence C., and Bruce I. Oppenheimer. *Congress Reconsidered.* 4th ed. Washington, D.C.: CQ Press, 1989.

Drew, Elizabeth. *Politics and Money: The New Road to Corruption.* New York: Macmillan, 1983.

Eismeier, Theodore J., and Philip H. Pollock III. *Business, Money and the Rise of Corporate PACs in American Elections.* New York: Quorum Books, 1988.

Federal Election Commission. "Annual Report." Washington, D.C., 1974.

——. "FEC Disclosure Series." Washington, D.C., 1975-76.

——. "FEC Reports on Financial Activities." Washington, D.C., 1977-78.

Goldenberg, Edie N., and Michael W. Traugott. *Campaigning for Congress.* Washington, D.C.: CQ Press, 1984.

Goldstein, Joshua. *The Fat Cats' Laundromat: Soft Money and the National Parties 1989-1990.* Washington, D.C.: Center for Responsive Politics, 1991.

Heard, Alexander. *The Costs of Democracy.* Chapel Hill: University of North Carolina Press, 1960.

Herrnson, Paul S. *Party Campaigning in the 1980s.* Cambridge, Mass.: Harvard University Press, 1988.

House Democratic Study Group. "Growing Dependence on Big Contributors." Special Rept. No. 101-33, July 30, 1990.

Huckabee, David C., and Joseph E. Cantor. "House Campaign Expenditures: 1980-1988." Rept. No. 89-534 GOV. Congressional Research Service, Library of Congress, September 20, 1989.

——. "Senate Campaign Expenditures, Receipts, and Sources of Funds: 1980-1990." Rept. No. 91-406 GOV. Washington, D.C.: Library of Congress, Congressional Research Service, May 8, 1991.

Jackson, Brooks. *Honest Graft: Big Money and the American Political Process.* New York: Knopf, 1988.

Jacobson, Gary C. *Money in Congressional Elections.* New Haven, Conn.: Yale University Press, 1980.

——. *The Politics of Congressional Elections.* 2nd ed. Boston: Little, Brown, 1987.

Makinson, Larry. *PACs in Profile: Industry and Interest Group Spending in the 1990 Elections.* Washington, D.C.: Center for Responsive Politics, 1991.

———. *The Price of Admission: An Illustrated Atlas of Campaign Spending in the 1988 Congressional Elections.* Washington, D.C.: Center for Responsive Politics, 1989.

———. *Open Secrets: The Dollar Power of PACs in Congress.* Washington, D.C.: Center for Responsive Politics/Congressional Quarterly, 1990.

Magleby, David B., and Candice J. Nelson. *The Money Chase: Congressional Campaign Finance Reform.* Washington, D.C.: Brookings Institution, 1990.

Malbin, Michael J., ed. *Money and Politics in the United States: Financing Elections in the 1980s.* Chatham, N.J.: Chatham House/American Enterprise Institute for Public Policy Research, 1984.

———. *Parties, Interest Groups, and Campaign Finance Laws.* Washington, D.C.: American Enterprise Institute for Public Policy Research, 1980.

Matasar, Ann B. *Corporate PACs and Federal Campaign Financing Laws: Use or Abuse of Power?* New York: Quorum Books, 1986.

Mutch, Robert E. *Campaigns, Congress, and Courts: The Making of Federal Campaign Finance Law.* New York: Praeger, 1988.

Nugent, Margaret Latus, and John R. Johannes. *Money, Elections, and Democracy: Reforming Congressional Campaign Finance.* Boulder, Colo.: Westview, 1990.

Ornstein, Norman J., Thomas E. Mann, and Michael J. Malbin. *Vital Statistics on Congress, 1991-1992.* Washington, D.C.: Congressional Quarterly, 1992.

Overacker, Louise. *Money in Elections.* New York: Macmillan, 1932.

Pollock, James K. *Party Campaign Funds.* New York: Knopf, 1926.

Sabato, Larry J. *PAC Power: Inside the World of Political Action Committees.* New York: W. W. Norton, 1984.

———. *The Party's Just Begun: Shaping Political Parties for America's Future.* Boston: Scott, Foresman/Little, Brown, 1988.

———. *Paying for Elections: The Campaign Finance Thicket.* New York: Priority Press/Twentieth Century Fund, 1989.

Shinn, Rinn-Sup. "Campaign Financing: National Public Opinion Polls." Rept. No. 91-346 GOV. Congressional Research Service, Library of Congress, April 12, 1991.

Sorauf, Frank J. *Money in American Elections.* Glenview, Ill.: Scott, Foresman/Little, Brown, 1988.

Thayer, George. *Who Shakes the Money Tree? American Campaign Financing from 1789 to the Present.* New York: Simon and Schuster, 1973.

INDEX

Our
Wet
World

Aquatic Ecosystems

Sneed B. Collard III
Illustrated by James M. Needham

ini Charlesbridge

Published by Charlesbridge Publishing
85 Main Street, Watertown, MA 02472
(617) 926-0329
www.charlesbridge.com

Library of Congress Cataloging-in-Publication Data
Collard, Sneed B.
    Our wet world / by Sneed B. Collard III; illustrated by
James M. Needham.
        p. cm.
    Summary: Describes the lives and interaction of animals
and plants that inhabit the many worlds of water.
    ISBN 0-88106-267-7 (reinforced for library use)
    ISBN 0-88106-268-5 (softcover)
    1. Aquatic organisms—Juvenile literature. 2. Aquatic ecology—
Juvenile literature. 3. Wetland ecology—Juvenile literature.
[1. Aquatic ecology. 2. Ecology.] I. Needham, James, ill. II. Title.
QH90.16.C65   1998
578.76—dc21   97-11873

Printed in the United States of America
(hc) 10 9 8 7 6 5 4 3 2
(sc) 10 9 8 7 6 5 4 3 2

For Mom, who gave me a life by the sea
—S. B. C. III

For those who love to watch waves . . .
—J. M. N.

Metric equivalents are approximate throughout the book.

The paintings in this book were done in gouache on Crescent illustration board.
The display type and text type were set in Usherwood.
Color separations were made by Eastern Rainbow, Inc., Derry, New Hampshire.
Printed and bound by Worzalla Publishing Company, Stevens Point, Wisconsin
This book was printed on recycled paper.
Production supervision by Brian G. Walker
Designed by Diane M. Earley

THE WORLD OF WET

Don't look now, but we're surrounded. Yes, you and I are surrounded by the most abundant liquid on earth—water.

Without water, we would dry up and blow away. Think about your body. Did you know that it is over 70 percent water? Or that you need to take in about two quarts of water each day to survive? You're not alone. Every plant and animal on the planet needs water to live, grow, and reproduce. But for over 250,000 kinds of living things, water fills an extra need. For them, water is home. Another name for these homes is *ecosystems.*

To explore some of earth's most fascinating watery, or *aquatic,* ecosystems, let's take a swim. Put on your mask, snorkel, and flippers and dive in.

STREAMS AND RIVERS

Streams and rivers are flowing freshwater ecosystems. They can be small, spring-fed creeks or powerful waterways such as the Mississippi River. They can be clear or murky, cold or warm.

In streams and rivers, flowing water always tugs at plants and animals. Water plants avoid being swept away by gripping the gravel or mud with their roots. Snails, worms, and crayfish keep from being carried away by hugging river and stream bottoms.

This stream is in the Rocky Mountains.

Rainbow trout are some of the largest animals in clear mountain streams. They are strong swimmers and can swim against the flowing water. Trout snatch up smaller fish or insect *larvae* to eat. Even a mayfly is not safe. Rainbow trout have excellent eyesight and can leap out of the water to snatch a fluttering treat.

PONDS AND LAKES

Ponds and lakes are also fresh water, but they are not in a hurry like a rushing stream or river. Water moves slowly in ponds and lakes, like the swirling liquid in an aquarium or swimming pool.

In these ecosystems, tiny floating plants use sunlight and *nutrients* to grow and multiply. Tiny animals graze on these plants. Together, these plants and animals are called *plankton*.

plankton

Plankton means "drifter," but not all life drifts about here. Insect larvae, shrimp, and small fish hunt for plankton to eat. Pickerel, bass, and sunfish chase smaller fish. On the bottom, a small worm wriggles next to a slimy rock. Wait. That's not a worm. It's not a rock, either. It's a 200-pound (90-kilogram) alligator snapping turtle wagging the pink end of its tongue. That hungry minnow better look somewhere else for a meal!

This pond is in the midwestern United States.

THE SALT MARSH

Salt marshes are quiet, muddy places next to the sea. Ocean tides rise and fall over them every day. Plants such as cordgrass and glassworts are the heroes of the salt marsh. These plants drink their water salty, not fresh. This enables them to live where land plants cannot survive.

Salt marsh plants trap mud and nutrients along the shore. They help hold the coastline together against waves and tides and give life to countless creatures. Northern harriers hunt for mice in the marsh while the rare clapper rail teaches its chicks to catch fiddler crabs.

This salt marsh is along the coast of Massachusetts during low tide.

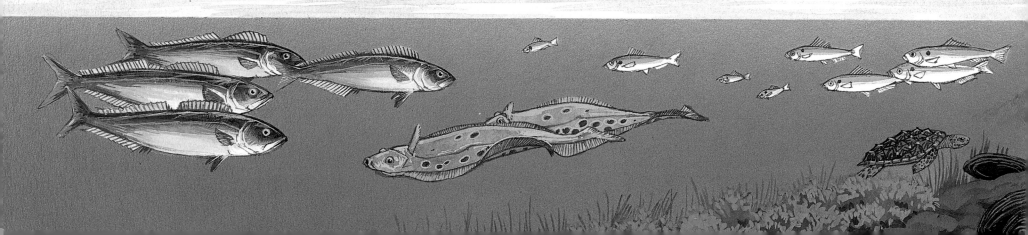

The plants also act as nurseries for baby fish of many kinds. These "fishlets" find shelter in the salt marsh and grow fat feeding in the nutrient-rich waters. Baby bluefish, flounder, and menhaden will grow into bigger fish that people like to catch.

THE MANGROVE FOREST

Not all muddy coastlines are covered by salt marsh plants. Close to the equator, you can find bushes and even trees up to 120 feet (37 meters) tall. These plants are called mangroves. Like salt marsh plants, mangroves are flooded by ocean tides every day. Mangrove mud has little oxygen in it, but the unusual prop roots of the mangroves allow the plants to breathe. Mangroves also have special salt glands in their leaves that get rid of extra sea salt.

This mangrove forest is on the coast of Papua New Guinea.

A "rain" of dead mangrove leaves nourishes a web of life here, starting with leaf-eating worms and brightly colored crabs. With its bulging eyes, the mudskipper looks like a space alien, but it is really a fish. During low tides, it walks or hops across the mud, snapping up insects and crabs. This fish breathes air and can even climb trees. That could come in handy when one of earth's most awesome predators—a saltwater crocodile—is nearby!

This rocky shore is on the coast of British Columbia, Canada.

THE ROCKY SHORE

CRASH! BOOM! SPLASH! Here, rocks—not mud—line the coast. Ocean tides rise and fall over these rocks each day. Unlike in the salt marsh and mangrove forest, swirling, crashing waves pound the rocky shore, so plants and animals have to hold on tight.

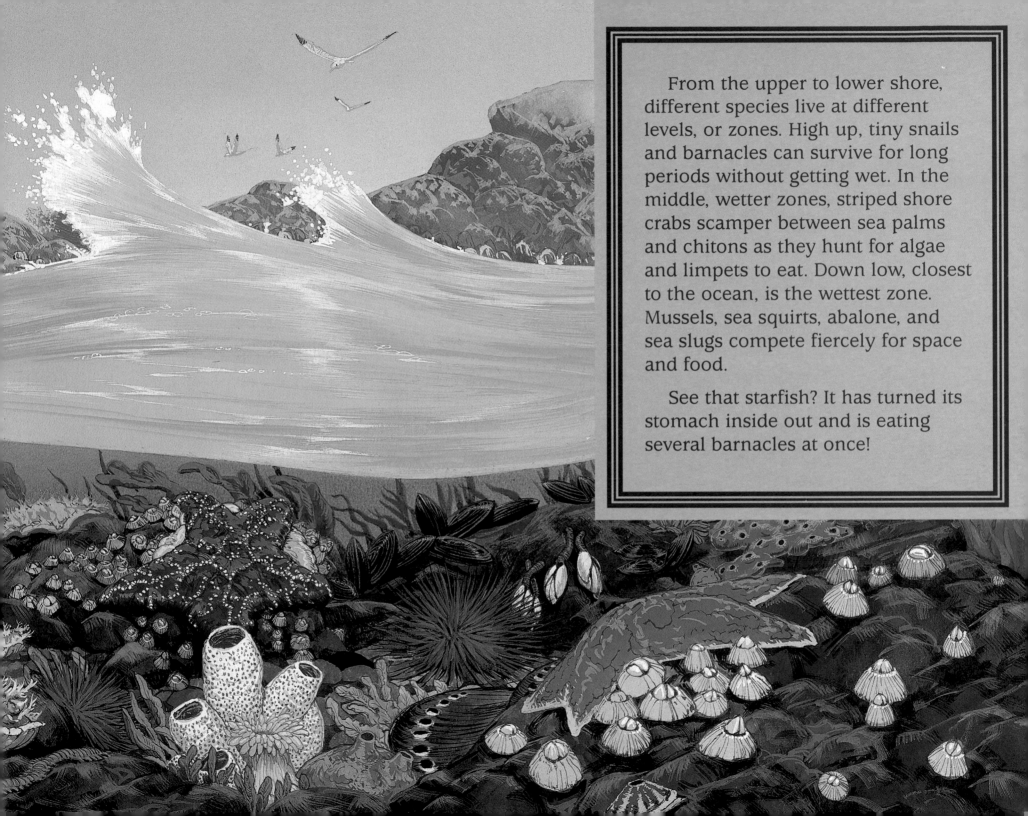

From the upper to lower shore, different species live at different levels, or zones. High up, tiny snails and barnacles can survive for long periods without getting wet. In the middle, wetter zones, striped shore crabs scamper between sea palms and chitons as they hunt for algae and limpets to eat. Down low, closest to the ocean, is the wettest zone. Mussels, sea squirts, abalone, and sea slugs compete fiercely for space and food.

See that starfish? It has turned its stomach inside out and is eating several barnacles at once!

THE KELP FOREST

Beyond the rocky shore, in cool shallow coastal waters, lives an undersea forest. The "trees" are brown algae called kelp. The largest kelp is the giant kelp. It grows over 140 feet (43 meters) long. Like land plants, kelp use the sun's energy to grow. During spring and summer, some kelp plants grow up to 14 inches (36 centimeters) per day!

This kelp forest is off the coast of northern California.

Kelp anchor themselves in place with rootlike *holdfasts*. Holdfasts are mini "apartment buildings" for tube worms, eels, and brittle stars. Cleverly camouflaged kelp crabs and kelp fish live higher up in the kelp, where sea otters come swooshing by. Some fishermen do not like sea otters because they eat sea urchins that the fishermen would like to catch. However, hungry sea urchins mow down new kelp plants. Without sea otters to eat these spiny "lawn mowers," the kelp forests—and the animals that live here—might soon disappear.

THE SEAGRASS MEADOW

Kelp forests do not grow in all shallow waters. Some shallows are covered by "prairies" of green plants called seagrasses. No buffalo graze on seagrasses, but hungry sea turtles, pinfish, and manatees do. Manatees are often called "sea cows." It's not hard to figure out why. They weigh up to 3,600 pounds (1,630 kilograms) and eat up to one-quarter of their body weights each day.

Besides feeding wildlife, seagrass meadows help clean up water by trapping particles of dirt and pollution. Like salt marshes, they act as safe hideouts for hundreds of species of fish, from sea horses to baby barracuda. Along the Gulf of Mexico, mullet, red drum, spotted seatrout, and most other fish that people eat spend at least part of their lives in these undersea grasslands.

This seagrass meadow is off the coast of southern Florida.

THE CORAL REEF

Dazzling living jewels fill the warm, shallow seas of the *tropics*. In the clear sunlit waters, large colonies of animals called corals have built underwater walls and platforms known as reefs. The reefs are made from the hard bony skeletons of the corals. As some corals die, others grow on top of them until spectacular underwater "cities" have formed.

This is the world's largest coral reef, the Great Barrier Reef in Australia.

Coral reefs are among the world's oldest ecosystems. In and around them are more kinds of life than anywhere else in the sea. Over 2,000 different kinds of brightly colored fish can be found around some coral reefs. So can three-foot-long (one-meter) giant clams with blue "lips." Giant clams look as though they could trap a person between their two shells, but don't worry—a clam can barely give a person a squeeze.

THE CONTINENTAL SHELF

Kelp forests, seagrass meadows, and many coral reefs all sit on shallow parts of the ocean along the edges of continents. These shallow areas are called continental shelves, and they are the sea's richest regions. Rivers carry loads of nutrients into shelf waters from the land. Other nutrients are brought by deep ocean currents rising to the surface. These nutrients feed great "blooms" of planktonic plants.

Plankton produce over half of the world's oxygen. They are food for dense schools of mackerel, herring, and cod. Over 90 percent of the fish people eat live on continental shelves. So do many of the most feared creatures in the ocean—sharks. Sharks are fish that have earned a bad reputation, but very few of them attack people. Most sharks eat smaller fish and help keep the continental shelf ecosystem balanced and healthy.

This is the continental shelf off the New England coast.

THE OPEN OCEAN or EPIPELAGIC ZONE

Far from land, the water is so clear that light reaches down hundreds of feet. Fewer animals live here than over the continental shelf because there is less food to eat. Still, the open ocean is not deserted. Comb jellies, sea butterflies, and giant salps sweep up plankton with their tentacles and sticky mucous nets.

This is the epipelagic zone in the tropical waters of the Pacific Ocean.

The jelly animals make fine dining for ten-foot (three-meter) leatherback sea turtles and 3,000-pound (1,360-kilogram) ocean sunfish, or mola molas.

Bluefin tuna are the "speedboats" of the epipelagic zone, and they are one of the only fish that is warm-blooded. This helps their muscles work very efficiently. They can race up to 50 miles (80 kilometers) per hour in search of anchovies, red crabs, and squid to eat. People have caught so many of these fish that they are now endangered.

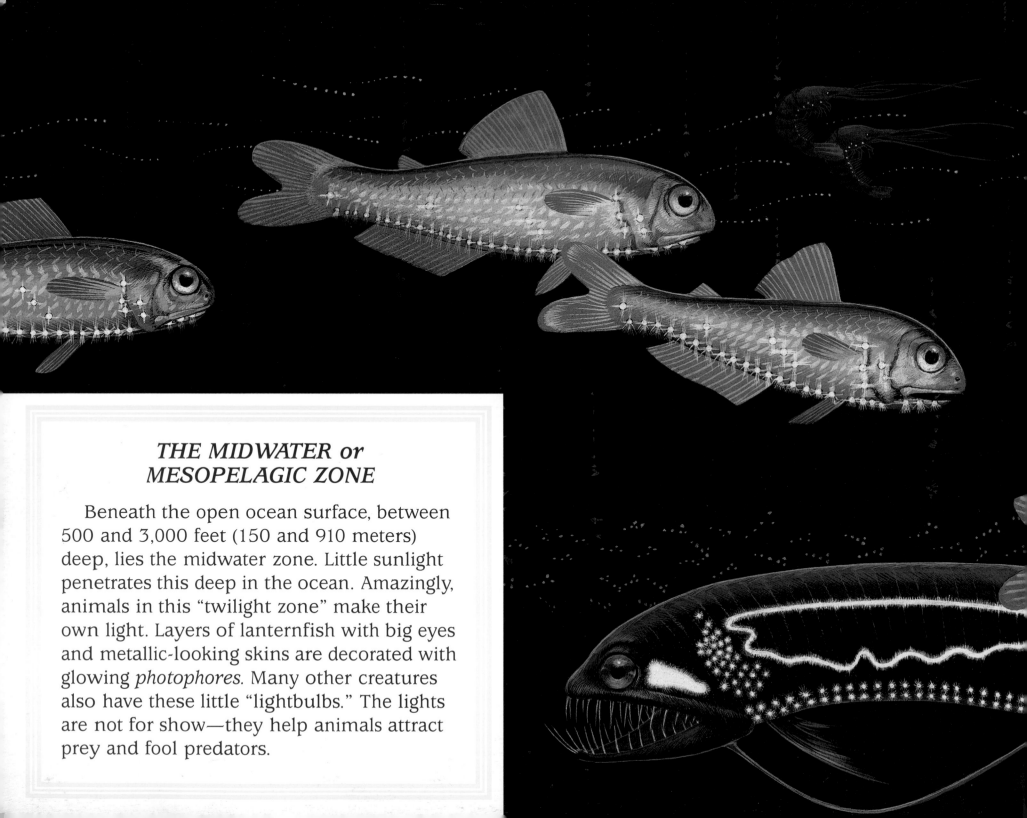

THE MIDWATER or MESOPELAGIC ZONE

Beneath the open ocean surface, between 500 and 3,000 feet (150 and 910 meters) deep, lies the midwater zone. Little sunlight penetrates this deep in the ocean. Amazingly, animals in this "twilight zone" make their own light. Layers of lanternfish with big eyes and metallic-looking skins are decorated with glowing *photophores*. Many other creatures also have these little "lightbulbs." The lights are not for show—they help animals attract prey and fool predators.

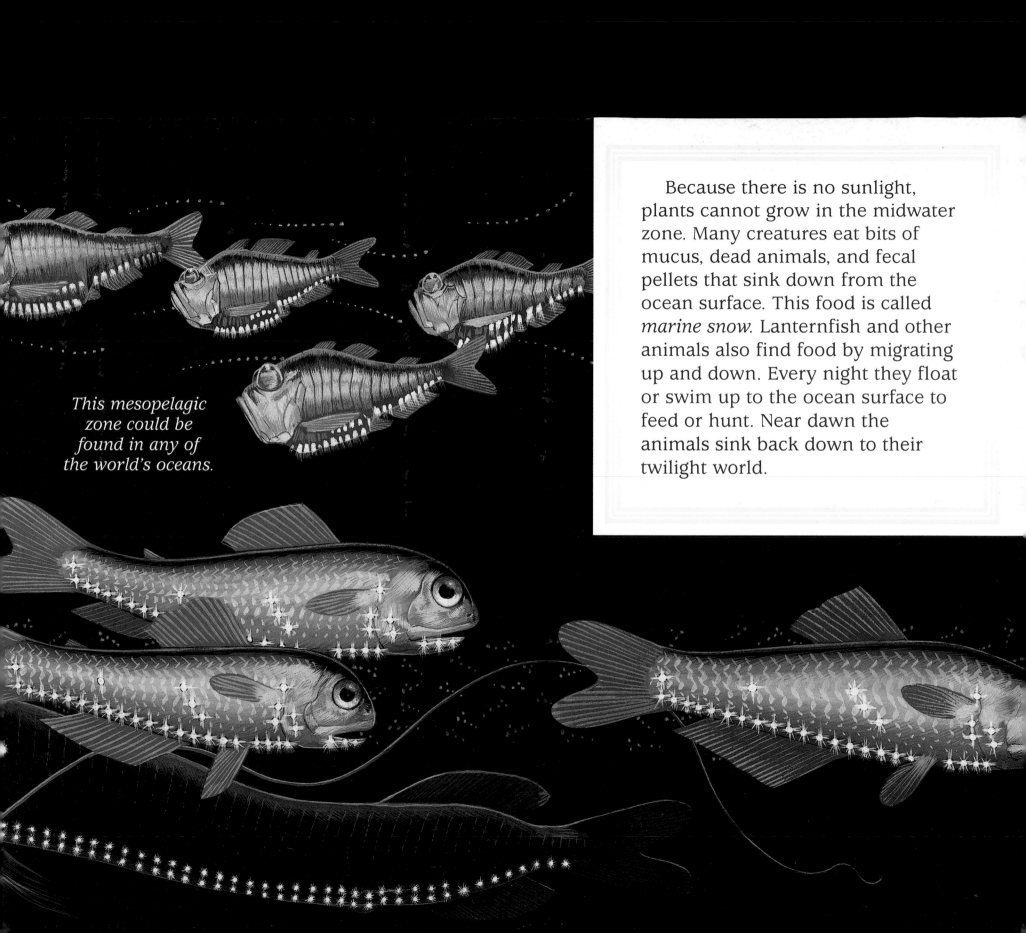

This mesopelagic zone could be found in any of the world's oceans.

Because there is no sunlight, plants cannot grow in the midwater zone. Many creatures eat bits of mucus, dead animals, and fecal pellets that sink down from the ocean surface. This food is called *marine snow*. Lanternfish and other animals also find food by migrating up and down. Every night they float or swim up to the ocean surface to feed or hunt. Near dawn the animals sink back down to their twilight world.

THE DEEP SEA or BATHYPELAGIC ZONE

One . . . two . . . three miles below the ocean surface lies the ocean floor. This is the deep sea, and it is the largest ecosystem on earth. The water is cold here—just above freezing. Water pressure is 1,000 times what it is at the surface and would crush most submarines. Over most of the sea bottom, big animals are rare. Big-eyed rattail fish are the most common fish that live here. They hunt smaller fish and sift through the bottom ooze for worms.

This deep-sea vent in the bathypelagic zone is on the bottom of the Pacific Ocean.

Where the earth's crust is spreading apart, hot water leaks into the ocean from under the ocean floor. These hot *deep-sea vents* support surprising "gardens" of life. Mussels, shrimp, and limpets feast on special bacteria that grow here. Most amazing are the five-foot-long (150-centimeter) *vestimentiferans*. They look like roses, but they are actually a kind of giant tube worm.

THE SOUTHERN OCEAN
or ANTARCTIC

Each winter, the Southern Ocean, or Antarctic, is plunged into darkness, and great ice sheets cover the ocean surface. Plankton stop growing, and fish make their own antifreeze, which keeps them from becoming "fish cubes" of ice. In the summer life flourishes. Thirty-eight kinds of penguins and other birds come to the Antarctic to feast and hatch new babies. They are joined by six kinds of seals and over fifteen kinds of whales.

The main meals for many animals are two-inch (five-centimeter) shrimplike animals called krill. They swim in schools up to a half-mile (800 meters) across. Between fifteen and thirty million crabeater seals munch on krill. So do penguins, fish, squid, and the largest creatures on earth—blue whales. The Southern Ocean is so important for marine mammals that the nations of the world have declared most of it a sanctuary for whales.

krill

These marine animals are in the Southern Ocean off the coast of Antarctica.

THE WET FRONTIER

Our wet world is not only fascinating—it's a key part of who we are. Over three billion years ago, life began in vast, ancient seas. Today water covers over 70 percent of the earth's surface and makes up nine-tenths of the living space on our planet.

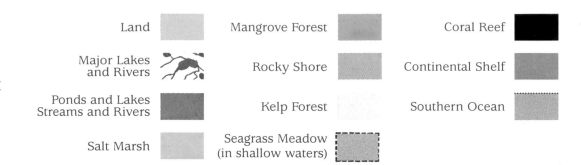

Land

Major Lakes and Rivers

Ponds and Lakes Streams and Rivers

Salt Marsh

Mangrove Forest

Rocky Shore

Kelp Forest

Seagrass Meadow (in shallow waters)

Coral Reef

Continental Shelf

Southern Ocean

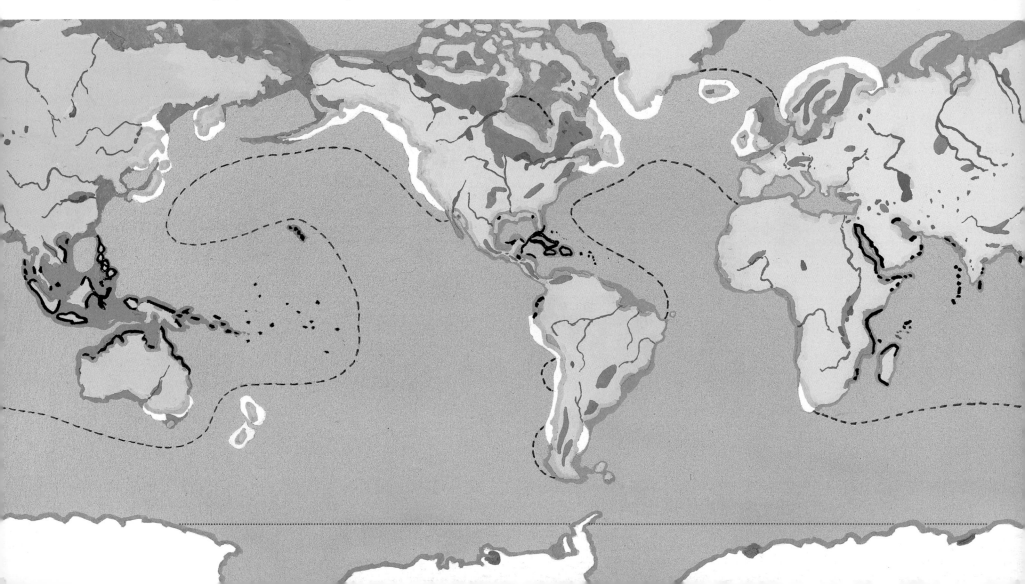

30 feet
(9 meters)

150 feet
(46 meters)

300 feet
(91 meters)

600 feet
(180 meters)

2,000 feet
(610 meters)

3,000 feet
(910 meters)

15,000 feet
(4600 meters)

epipelagic zone

mesopelagic zone

bathypelagic zone

Map scale varies with depth.

The underwater world often seems strange to us, but we depend on it for water, oxygen, food, energy, transportation— even fun! Today you swam through several of the most spectacular watery places on earth. But your swim was just a beginning. Other underwater places await your exploration and, with them, thousands of creatures we couldn't fit in this book.

Scientists have a great deal to learn about our watery world, too. Many more discoveries lie ahead. They promise to excite us and help us protect the wet planet that we call home.

GLOSSARY

aquatic: something that is living on or in the water.

continental shelf: the edge of a continent that is covered by water, usually to a maximum depth of about 650 feet (200 meters). Kelp forests, seagrass meadows, and some coral reefs are found on the shallower parts of continental shelves.

coral reef: a formation made of the skeletons of coral colonies, found in shallow, clear tropical seas usually less than 100 feet (30 meters) deep.

deep-sea or bathypelagic zone: the ocean floor beyond the continental shelf and slope, usually at a depth greater than 3000 feet (910 meters).

deep-sea vent: a place on the ocean floor where hot water seeps into the ocean. Most vents are located where the earth's tectonic plates are spreading apart. Many are surrounded by life-forms that live nowhere else.

ecosystem: a community of living things and their physical environment.

holdfast: the rootlike structure by which algae attach themselves to rocks, sea bottoms, and other surfaces.

kelp forest: a concentrated group of brown algae growing on shallow sandy or rocky bottoms near the shore. The giant kelp of the Pacific Ocean can grow up to 140 feet (43 meters) long.

larva: the early form of an animal that is different from the adult form. It must undergo a change, or metamorphosis, to become an adult.

mangrove forest: a community of bush- or treelike plants called "mangroves" that live in coastal, tropical areas. Like salt marsh plants, mangroves are known for their ability to live in muddy soils and to tolerate salt water.

marine snow: clumps and "flakes" consisting of mucus, feces, bacteria, and various body parts of marine animals. Marine snow sinks from upper ocean layers and serves as food for animals living in the deeper regions of the ocean.

midwater or mesopelagic zone: the area of the ocean between about 500 and 3,000 feet (about 150 and 910 meters) deep. Very little light penetrates here, giving this zone a "twilight" appearance.

nutrient: something that provides food or nourishment, usually a mineral such as nitrogen or phosphorus.

open ocean or epipelagic zone: the top, usually clear layer of open ocean where sunlight penetrates. It usually extends down to about 500 feet (about 150 meters).

photophore: a light-producing organ found on many kinds of fish and other animals.

plankton: plants, animals, and other living things that float or drift in great numbers in rivers, lakes, oceans, and other bodies of water. Most are very small but some, such as jellyfish and ocean sunfish, can be quite large.

ponds and lakes: still or slow-moving bodies of water that are found inland, away from the ocean. Ponds are usually much smaller than lakes.

rocky shore: a coastline composed of rock or other hard substances that are covered and uncovered by ocean tides. Rocky shores are noted for having distinct zones that contain different plants and animals.

salt marsh: a mudflat found in shallow quiet waters along bays or behind barrier islands, settled by animals and salt-tolerant plants.

seagrass meadow: a bed or field of grasslike, flowering plants in shallow coastal waters, usually with a soft sandy or muddy bottom.

Southern Ocean: the ocean that surrounds Antarctica. It merges with the Indian, Atlantic, and Pacific Oceans at about 60 degrees south latitude.

streams and rivers: bodies of fresh water that usually flow into oceans, lakes, or other rivers.

tropics: the region of the earth from 23½ degrees latitude north of the equator to 23½ degrees south of the equator. This part of our planet receives more sunlight than any other and is therefore the warmest part of the globe.

vestimentiferans: a kind of brightly colored tube worm found living near deep-sea vents.